FREOffer

To help us better serve yoit we would like to give you for FREE. **This DVD covers world-class test taking tips that you can use to be even more successful when you are taking your test.**

All that we ask is that you email us your feedback about your study guide. Please let us know what you thought about it – whether that is good, bad or indifferent.

To get your **FREE Test Taking Tips DVD**, email freedvd@studyguideteam.com with "FREE DVD" in the subject line and the following information in the body of the email:

    a. The title of your study guide.

    b. Your product rating on a scale of 1-5, with 5 being the highest rating.

    c. Your feedback about the study guide. What did you think of it?

    d. Your full name and shipping address to send your free DVD.

If you have any questions or concerns, please don't hesitate to contact us at freedvd@studyguideteam.com.

Thanks again!

ACCUPLACER Study Guide

ACCUPLACER Test Prep Team

Table of Contents

Quick Overview

As you draw closer to taking your exam, effective preparation becomes more and more important. Thankfully, you have this study guide to help you get ready. Use this guide to help keep your studying on track and refer to it often.

This study guide contains several key sections that will help you be successful on your exam. The guide contains tips for what you should do the night before and the day of the test. Also included are test-taking tips. Knowing the right information is not always enough. Many well-prepared test takers struggle with exams. These tips will help equip you to accurately read, assess, and answer test questions.

A large part of the guide is devoted to showing you what content to expect on the exam and to helping you better understand that content. Near the end of this guide is a practice test so that you can see how well you have grasped the content. Then, answers explanations are provided so that you can understand why you missed certain questions.

Don't try to cram the night before you take your exam. This is not a wise strategy for a few reasons. First, your retention of the information will be low. Your time would be better used by reviewing information you already know rather than trying to learn a lot of new information. Second, you will likely become stressed as you try to gain large amount of knowledge in a short amount of time. Third, you will be depriving yourself of sleep. So be sure to go to bed at a reasonable time the night before. Being well-rested helps you focus and remain calm.

Be sure to eat a substantial breakfast the morning of the exam. If you are taking the exam in the afternoon, be sure to have a good lunch as well. Being hungry is distracting and can make it difficult to focus. You have hopefully spent lots of time preparing for the exam. Don't let an empty stomach get in the way of success!

When travelling to the testing center, leave earlier than needed. That way, you have a buffer in case you experience any delays. This will help you remain calm and will keep you from missing your appointment time at the testing center.

Be sure to pace yourself during the exam. Don't try to rush through the exam. There is no need to risk performing poorly on the exam just so you can leave the testing center early. Allow yourself to use all of the allotted time if needed.

Remain positive while taking the exam even if you feel like you are performing poorly. Thinking about the content you should have mastered will not help you perform better on the exam.

Once the exam is complete, take some time to relax. Even if you feel that you need to take the exam again, you will be well served by some down time before you begin studying again. It's often easier to convince yourself to study if you know that it will come with a reward!

Test-Taking Strategies

1. Predicting the Answer

When you feel confident in your preparation for a multiple-choice test, try predicting the answer before reading the answer choices. This is especially useful on questions that test objective factual knowledge or that ask you to fill in a blank. By predicting the answer before reading the available choices, you eliminate the possibility that you will be distracted or led astray by an incorrect answer choice. You will feel more confident in your selection if you read the question, predict the answer, and then find your prediction among the answer choices. After using this strategy, be sure to still read all of the answer choices carefully and completely. If you feel unprepared, you should not attempt to predict the answers. This would be a waste of time and an opportunity for your mind to wander in the wrong direction.

2. Reading the Whole Question

Too often, test takers scan a multiple-choice question, recognize a few familiar words, and immediately jump to the answer choices. Test authors are aware of this common impatience, and they will sometimes prey upon it. For instance, a test author might subtly turn the question into a negative, or he or she might redirect the focus of the question right at the end. The only way to avoid falling into these traps is to read the entirety of the question carefully before reading the answer choices.

3. Looking for Wrong Answers

Long and complicated multiple-choice questions can be intimidating. One way to simplify a difficult multiple-choice question is to eliminate all of the answer choices that are clearly wrong. In most sets of answers, there will be at least one selection that can be dismissed right away. If the test is administered on paper, the test taker could draw a line through it to indicate that it may be ignored; otherwise, the test taker will have to perform this operation mentally or on scratch paper. In either case, once the obviously incorrect answers have been eliminated, the remaining choices may be considered. Sometimes identifying the clearly wrong answers will give the test taker some information about the correct answer. For instance, if one of the remaining answer choices is a direct opposite of one of the eliminated answer choices, it may well be the correct answer. The opposite of obviously wrong is obviously right! Of course, this is not always the case. Some answers are obviously incorrect simply because they are irrelevant to the question being asked. Still, identifying and eliminating some incorrect answer choices is a good way to simplify a multiple-choice question.

4. Don't Overanalyze

Anxious test takers often overanalyze questions. When you are nervous, your brain will often run wild causing you to make associations and discover clues that don't actually exist. If you feel that this may be a problem for you, do whatever you can to slow down during the test. Try taking a deep breath or counting to ten. As you read and consider the question, restrict yourself to the particular words used by the author. Avoid thought tangents about what the author *really* meant, or what he or she was *trying* to say. The only things that matter on a multiple-choice test are the words that are actually in the question. You must avoid reading too much into a multiple-choice question, or supposing that the writer meant something other than what he or she wrote.

5. No Need for Panic

It is wise to learn as many strategies as possible before taking a multiple-choice test, but it is likely that you will come across a few questions for which you simply don't know the answer. In this situation, avoid panicking. Because most multiple-choice tests include dozens of questions, the relative value of a single wrong answer is small. Moreover, your failure on one question has no effect on your success elsewhere on the test. As much as possible, you should compartmentalize each question on a multiple-choice test. In other words, you should not allow your feelings about one question to affect your success on the others. When you find a question that you either don't understand or don't know how to answer, just take a deep breath and do your best. Read the entire question slowly and carefully. Try rephrasing the question a couple of different ways. Then, read all of the answer choices carefully. After eliminating obviously wrong answers, make a selection and move on to the next question.

6. Confusing Answer Choices

When working on a difficult multiple-choice question, there may be a tendency to focus on the answer choices that are the easiest to understand. Many people, whether consciously or not, gravitate to the answer choices that require the least concentration, knowledge, and memory. This is a mistake. When you come across an answer choice that is confusing, you need to give it extra attention. A question might be confusing because you do not know the subject matter to which it refers. If this is the case, don't eliminate the answer before you have affirmatively settled on another. When you come across an answer choice of this type, set it aside as you look at the remaining choices. If you can confidently assert that one of the other choices is correct, you can leave the confusing answer aside. Otherwise, you will need to take a moment to try to better understand the confusing answer choice. Rephrasing is one way to tease out the sense of a confusing answer choice.

7. Your First Instinct

Many people struggle with multiple-choice tests because they overthink the questions. If you have studied sufficiently for the test, you should be prepared to trust your first instinct once you have carefully and completely read the question and all of the answer choices. There is a great deal of research suggesting that the mind can come to the correct conclusion very quickly once it has obtained all of the relevant information. At times, it may seem to you as if your intuition is working faster even than your reasoning mind. This may in fact be true. The knowledge you obtain while studying may be retrieved from your subconscious before you have a chance to work out the associations that support it. Verify your instinct by working out the reasons that it should be trusted.

8. Key Words

Many test takers struggle with multiple-choice questions because they have poor reading comprehension skills. Quickly reading and understanding a multiple-choice question requires a mixture of skill and experience. To help with this, try jotting down a few key words and phrases on a piece of scrap paper. Doing this concentrates the process of reading and forces the mind to weigh the relative importance of the question's parts. In selecting words and phrases to write down, the test taker thinks about the question more deeply and carefully. This is especially true for multiple-choice questions that are preceded by a long prompt.

9. Subtle Negatives

One of the oldest tricks in the multiple-choice test writer's book is to subtly reverse the meaning of a question with a word like *not* or *except*. If you are not paying attention to each word in the question, you can easily be led astray by this trick. For instance, a common question format is, "Which of the following is...?" Obviously, if the question instead is, "Which of the following is not....?," then the answer will be quite different. Even worse, the test makers are aware of the potential for this mistake and will include one answer choice that would be correct if the question were not negated or reversed. A test taker who misses the reversal will find what he or she believes to be a correct answer and will be so confident that he or she will fail to reread the question and discover the original error. The only way to avoid this is to practice a wide variety of multiple-choice questions and to pay close attention to each and every word.

10. Reading Every Answer Choice

It may seem obvious, but you should always read every one of the answer choices! Too many test takers fall into the habit of scanning the question and assuming that they understand the question because they recognize a few key words. From there, they pick the first answer choice that answers the question they believe they have read. Test takers who read all of the answer choices might discover that one of the latter answer choices is actually *more* correct. Moreover, reading all of the answer choices can remind you of facts related to the question that can help you arrive at the correct answer. Sometimes, a misstatement or incorrect detail in one of the latter answer choices will trigger your memory of the subject and will enable you to find the right answer. Failing to read all of the answer choices is like not reading all of the items on a restaurant menu: you might miss out on the perfect choice.

11. Spot the Hedges

One of the keys to success on multiple-choice tests is paying close attention to every word. This is never more true than with words like *almost*, *most*, *some*, and *sometimes*. These words are called "hedges", because they indicate that a statement is not totally true or not true in every place and time. An absolute statement will contain no hedges, but in many subjects, like literature and history, the answers are not always straightforward or absolute. There are always exceptions to the rules in these subjects. For this reason, you should favor those multiple-choice questions that contain hedging language. The presence of qualifying words indicates that the author is taking special care with his or her words, which is certainly important when composing the right answer. After all, there are many ways to be wrong, but there is only one way to be right! For this reason, it is wise to avoid answers that are absolute when taking a multiple-choice test. An absolute answer is one that says things are either all one way or all another. They often include words like *every*, *always*, *best*, and *never*. If you are taking a multiple-choice test in a subject that doesn't lend itself to absolute answers, be on your guard if you see any of these words.

12. Long Answers

In many subject areas, the answers are not simple. As already mentioned, the right answer often requires hedges. Another common feature of the answers to a complex or subjective question are qualifying clauses, which are groups of words that subtly modify the meaning of the sentence. If the question or answer choice describes a rule to which there are exceptions or the subject matter is complicated, ambiguous, or confusing, the correct answer will require many words in order to be expressed clearly and accurately. In essence, you should not be deterred by answer choices that seem excessively long. Oftentimes, the author of the text will not be able to write the correct answer without offering some qualifications and modifications. Your job is to read the answer choices thoroughly and completely and to select the one that most accurately and precisely answers the question.

13. Restating to Understand

Sometimes, a question on a multiple-choice test is difficult not because of what it asks but because of how it is written. If this is the case, restate the question or answer choice in different words. This process serves a couple of important purposes. First, it forces you to concentrate on the core of the question. In order to rephrase the question accurately, you have to understand it well. Rephrasing the question will concentrate your mind on the key words and ideas. Second, it will present the information to your mind in a fresh way. This process may trigger your memory and render some useful scrap of information picked up while studying.

14. True Statements

Sometimes an answer choice will be true in itself, but it does not answer the question. This is one of the main reasons why it is essential to read the question carefully and completely before proceeding to the answer choices. Too often, test takers skip ahead to the answer choices and look for true statements. Having found one of these, they are content to select it without reference to the question above. Obviously, this provides an easy way for test makers to play tricks. The savvy test taker will always read the entire question before turning to the answer choices. Then, having settled on a correct answer choice, he or she will refer to the original question and ensure that the selected answer is relevant. The mistake of choosing a correct-but-irrelevant answer choice is especially common on questions related to specific pieces of objective knowledge, like historical or scientific facts. A prepared test taker will have a wealth of factual knowledge at his or her disposal, and should not be careless in its application.

15. No Patterns

One of the more dangerous ideas that circulates about multiple-choice tests is that the correct answers tend to fall into patterns. These erroneous ideas range from a belief that B and C are the most common right answers, to the idea that an unprepared test-taker should answer "A-B-A-C-A-D-A-B-A." It cannot be emphasized enough that pattern-seeking of this type is exactly the WRONG way to approach a multiple-choice test. To begin with, it is highly unlikely that the test maker will plot the correct answers according to some predetermined pattern. The questions are scrambled and delivered in a random order. Furthermore, even if the test maker was following a pattern in the assignation of correct answers, there is no reason why the test taker would know which pattern he or she was using. Any attempt to discern a pattern in the answer choices is a waste of time and a distraction from the real work of taking the test. A test taker would be much better served by extra preparation before the test than by reliance on a pattern in the answers.

FREE DVD OFFER

Don't forget that doing well on your exam includes both understanding the test content and understanding how to use what you know to do well on the test. We offer a completely FREE Test Taking Tips DVD that covers world class test taking tips that you can use to be even more successful when you are taking your test.

All that we ask is that you email us your feedback about your study guide. To get your **FREE Test Taking Tips DVD**, email freedvd@studyguideteam.com with "FREE DVD" in the subject line and the following information in the body of the email:

- The title of your study guide.
- Your product rating on a scale of 1-5, with 5 being the highest rating.
- Your feedback about the study guide. What did you think of it?
- Your full name and shipping address to send your free DVD.

ACCUPLACER Introduction

Function of the Test

ACCUPLACER is an adaptive, computerized test offered by the College Board and used by some colleges and high schools to determine placement of students in programs appropriate to the students' skill level. The test is offered nation-wide, at any college or high school that chooses to use it. Test-takers are almost always students of schools that use the ACCUPLACER in their course selection and placement efforts. Schools can also use the ACCUPLACER to assess students' skill levels and identify specific areas in which the students need improvement. Scores are generally used only by the college or high school the student is already attending for placement and instruction at that school.

According to the College Board, more than 1,500 secondary and post-secondary institutions are currently using the ACCUPLACER. Over 7.5 million ACCUPLACER tests are administered in a typical year. The College Board recommends that ACCUPLACER scores be used in conjunction with other variables including high school GPA, the number of years a student has taken coursework in a particular subject area, other test scores such as the SAT or ACT, as well as non-cognitive information such as motivation, family support, and time management skills, in order to place students in courses of appropriate difficulty.

Test Administration

ACCUPLACER is offered by computer, usually by the school that wants to use its results, whenever a student makes an appointment with the school to take it. In cases where a student is not able to take the test at the student's school, arrangements can sometimes be made to take the test at a more convenient location on another school's campus.

Fees for taking the ACCUPLACER vary from school to school. Students sometimes do not pay a fee at all; rather, the school pays the College Board for the right to administer the test and then students take it for free. Students may retake the ACCUPLACER at the discretion of the school administering the test and using its results. Students with documented disabilities can make arrangements, through the test center offering the ACCUPLACER, to take the test with appropriate accommodations, including the potential availability of a written version of the test.

Test Format

The core of the ACCUPLACER is five multiple-choice subject area tests: Arithmetic, College-level Math, Elementary Algebra, Reading Comprehension, and Sentence Skills. A college may ask a student to test in any or all of the five subject areas, depending on the student's and the school's needs. There is also a sixth section, called the WritePlacer, in which students must write a brief essay. Finally, there are four multiple-choice ESL sections of the ACCUPLACER, which schools may ask students, for whom English is a second language, to take.

The multiple-choice sections of the ACCUPLACER are administered by computer. There is no time-limit, so test takers should feel free to work at their own pace. A typical test section might take around 30 minutes to complete. The test is adaptive, meaning it adjusts the difficulty of each question based on the student's success on the previous questions. The more questions a test-taker gets right, the harder succeeding questions will be and vice-versa. This allows the test to more readily determine test-takers' ability levels without wasting time on questions far above or far below what the test-takers can answer.

Section	Questions	Description
Arithmetic	17	Basic arithmetic and problem solving
College Level Math	20	Algebra, geometry, trigonometry
Elementary Algebra	12	Basic algebra
Reading Comprehension	20	Understanding reading; making inferences
Sentence Skills	20	Sentence structure; relationships between sentences
WritePlacer	1 essay	Effective written communication
ESL- Language Use	20	English grammar
ESL- Listening	20	Understanding spoken English communication
ESL- Reading Skills	20	Comprehension of short written English passages
ESL- Sentence Meaning	20	Understanding the meaning of English sentences

Scoring

The ACCUPLACER subject area tests are scored on a scale from 20 to 120. Schools are free to use the scores for placement as they see fit, given that the difficulty of coursework varies from school to school. A typical community college might separate scores into tiered groups from 50 to 75, from 75 to 99, and from 100 to 120. Scores are typically generated instantly by the computer, but may not be available from the school administering the test until the school has had a chance to review the scores and use them for placement purposes.

Recent/Future Developments

Starting in September 2016, the College Board will be making "next-generation" ACCUPLACER tests available to schools. Schools will have the option of administering the next-generation tests or the older tests, but not both. The new next-generation tests will include redesigned reading, writing, and math content, intended to more effectively help schools place students in classes that match their skill level.

Arithmetic

Addition with Whole Numbers and Fractions

Addition combines two quantities together. With whole numbers, this is taking two sets of things and merging them into one, then counting the result. For example, 4 + 3 = 7. When adding numbers, the order does not matter: 3 + 4 = 7, also. Longer lists of whole numbers can also be added together. The result of adding numbers is called the *sum*.

With fractions, the number on top is the *numerator*, and the number on the bottom is the *denominator*. To add fractions, the denominator must be the same—a *common denominator*. To find a common denominator, the existing numbers on the bottom must be considered, and the lowest number they will both multiply into must be determined. Consider the following equation:

$$\frac{1}{3} + \frac{5}{6} = ?$$

The numbers 3 and 6 both multiply into 6. Three can be multiplied by 2, and 6 can be multiplied by 1. The top and bottom of each fraction must be multiplied by the same number. Then, the numerators are added together to get a new numerator. The following equation is the result:

$$\frac{1}{3} + \frac{5}{6} = \frac{2}{6} + \frac{5}{6} = \frac{7}{6}$$

Subtraction with Whole Numbers and Fractions

Subtraction is taking one quantity away from another, so it is the opposite of addition. The expression 4 − 3 means taking 3 away from 4. So, 4 − 3 = 1. In this case, the order matters, since it entails taking one quantity away from the other, rather than just putting two quantities together. The result of subtraction is also called the *difference*.

To subtract fractions, the denominator must be the same. Then, subtract the numerators together to get a new numerator. Here is an example:

$$\frac{1}{3} - \frac{5}{6} = \frac{2}{6} - \frac{5}{6} = \frac{-3}{6} = -\frac{1}{2}$$

Multiplication with Whole Numbers and Fractions

Multiplication is a kind of repeated addition. The expression 4×5 is taking four sets, each of them having five things in them, and putting them all together. That means $4 \times 5 = 5 + 5 + 5 + 5 = 20$. As with addition, the order of the numbers does not matter. The result of a multiplication problem is called the *product*.

To multiply fractions, the numerators are multiplied to get the new numerator, and the denominators are multiplied to get the new denominator:

$$\frac{1}{3} \times \frac{5}{6} = \frac{1 \times 5}{3 \times 6} = \frac{5}{18}$$

When multiplying fractions, common factors can *cancel* or *divide into one another*, when factors that appear in the numerator of one fraction and the denominator of the other fraction. Here is an example:

$$\frac{1}{3} \times \frac{9}{8} = \frac{1}{1} \times \frac{3}{8} = 1 \times \frac{3}{8} = \frac{3}{8}$$

The numbers 3 and 9 have a common factor of 3, so that factor can be divided out.

Division with Whole Numbers and Fractions

Division is the opposite of multiplication. With whole numbers, it means splitting up one number into sets of equal size. For example, $16 \div 8$ is the number of sets of eight things that can be made out of sixteen things. Thus, $16 \div 8 = 2$. As with subtraction, the order of the numbers will make a difference, here. The answer to a division problem is called the *quotient*, while the number in front of the division sign is called the *dividend* and the number behind the division sign is called the *divisor*.

To divide fractions, the first fraction must be multiplied with the reciprocal of the second fraction. The *reciprocal* of the fraction $\frac{x}{y}$ is the fraction $\frac{y}{x}$. Here is an example:

$$\frac{1}{3} \div \frac{5}{6} = \frac{1}{3} \times \frac{6}{5} = \frac{6}{15} = \frac{2}{5}$$

Recognizing Equivalent Fractions and Mixed Numbers

The value of a fraction does not change if multiplying or dividing both the numerator and the denominator by the same number (other than 0). In other words, $\frac{x}{y} = \frac{a \times x}{a \times y} = \frac{x \div a}{y \div a}$, as long as a is not 0. This means that $\frac{2}{5} = \frac{4}{10}$, for example. If x and y are integers that have no common factors, then the fraction is said to be *simplified*. This means $\frac{2}{5}$ is simplified, but $\frac{4}{10}$ is not.

Often when working with fractions, the fractions need to be rewritten so that they all share a single denominator—this is called finding a *common denominator* for the fractions. Using two fractions, $\frac{a}{b}$ and $\frac{c}{d}$, the numerator and denominator of the left fraction can be multiplied by d, while the numerator and denominator of the right fraction can be multiplied by b. This provides the fractions $\frac{a \times d}{b \times d}$ and $\frac{c \times b}{d \times b}$ with the common denominator $b \times d$.

A fraction whose numerator is smaller than its denominator is called a *proper fraction*. A fraction whose numerator is bigger than its denominator is called an *improper fraction*. These numbers can be rewritten as a combination of integers and fractions, called a *mixed number*. For example, $\frac{6}{5} = \frac{5}{5} + \frac{1}{5} = 1 + \frac{1}{5}$, and can be written as $1\frac{1}{5}$.

Estimating

Estimation is finding a value that is close to a solution but is not the exact answer. For example, if there are values in the thousands to be multiplied, then each value can be estimated to the nearest thousand and the calculation performed. This value provides an approximate solution that can be determined very quickly.

Recognition of Decimals

The *decimal system* is a way of writing out numbers that uses ten different numerals: 0, 1, 2, 3, 4, 5, 6, 7, 8, and 9. This is also called a "base ten" or "base 10" system. Other bases are also used. For example, computers work with a base of 2. This means they only use the numerals 0 and 1.

The *decimal place* denotes how far to the right of the decimal point a numeral is. The first digit to the right of the decimal point is in the *tenths* place. The next is the *hundredths*. The third is the *thousandths*.

So, 3.142 has a 1 in the tenths place, a 4 in the hundredths place, and a 2 in the thousandths place.

The *decimal point* is a period used to separate the *ones* place from the *tenths* place when writing out a number as a decimal.

A *decimal number* is a number written out with a decimal point instead of as a fraction, for example, 1.25 instead of $\frac{5}{4}$. Depending on the situation, it can sometimes be easier to work with fractions and sometimes easier to work with decimal numbers.

A decimal number is *terminating* if it stops at some point. It is called *repeating* if it never stops, but repeats a pattern over and over. It is important to note that every rational number can be written as a terminating decimal or as a repeating decimal.

Addition with Decimals

To add decimal numbers, each number in columns needs to be lined up by the decimal point. For each number being added, the zeros to the right of the last number need to be filled in so that each of the numbers has the same number of places to the right of the decimal. Then, the columns can be added together. Here is an example of 2.45 + 1.3 + 8.891 written in column form:

$$2.450$$

$$1.300$$

$$+\ 8.891$$

Zeros have been added in the columns so that each number has the same number of places to the right of the decimal.

Added together, the correct answer is 12.641:

$$2.450$$

$$1.300$$

$$+\ 8.891$$

$$12.641$$

Subtraction with Decimals

Subtracting decimal numbers is the same process as adding decimals. Here is $7.89 - 4.235$ written in column form:

$$7.890$$

$$- \underline{4.235}$$

$$3.655$$

A zero has been added in the column so that each number has the same number of places to the right of the decimal.

Multiplication with Decimals

Decimals can be multiplied as if there were no decimals points in the problem. For example, 0.5 x 1.25 can be rewritten and multiplied as 5 x 125, which equals 625.

The final answer will have the same number of decimal *points* as the total number of decimal *places* in the problem. The first number has one decimal place, and the second number has two decimal places. Therefore, the final answer will contain three decimal places:

0.5 x 1.25 = 0.625

Division with Decimals

Dividing a decimal by a whole number entails using long division first by ignoring the decimal point. Then, the decimal point is moved the number of places given in the problem.

For example, $6.8 \div 4$ can be rewritten as $68 \div 4$, which is 17. There is one non-zero integer to the right of the decimal point, so the final solution would have one decimal place to the right of the solution. In this case, the solution is 1.7.

Dividing a decimal by another decimal requires changing the divisor to a whole number by moving its decimal point. The decimal place of the dividend should be moved by the same number of places as the divisor. Then, the problem is the same as dividing a decimal by a whole number.

For example, $5.72 \div 1.1$ has a divisor with one decimal point in the denominator. The expression can be rewritten as $57.2 \div 11$ by moving each number one decimal place to the right to eliminate the decimal. The long division can be completed as $572 \div 11$ with a result of 52. Since there is one non-zero integer to the right of the decimal point in the problem, the final solution is 5.2.

In another example, $8 \div 0.16$ has a divisor with two decimal points in the denominator. The expression can be rewritten as $800 \div 16$ by moving each number two decimal places to the right to eliminate the decimal in the divisor. The long division can be completed with a result of 50.

Fraction and Percent Equivalencies

The word *percent* comes from the Latin phrase for "per one hundred." A *percent* is a way of writing out a fraction. It is a fraction with a denominator of 100. Thus, $65\% = \frac{65}{100}$.

To convert a fraction to a percent, the denominator is written as 100. For example, $\frac{3}{5} = \frac{60}{100} = 60\%$.

In converting a percent to a fraction, the percent is written with a denominator of 100, and the result is simplified. For example, $30\% = \frac{30}{100} = \frac{3}{10}$.

Percent Problems

The basic percent equation is the following:

$$\frac{is}{of} = \frac{\%}{100}$$

The placement of numbers in the equation depends on what the question asks.

<u>Example 1</u>
Find 40% of 80.

Basically, the problem is asking, "What is 40% of 80?" The 40% is the percent, and 80 is the number to find the percent "of." The equation is:

$$\frac{x}{80} = \frac{40}{100}$$

Solving the equation by cross-multiplication, the problem becomes 100x = 80(40). Solving for x gives the answer: x = 32.

<u>Example 2</u>
What percent of 100 is 20?

The 20 fills in the "is" portion, while 100 fills in the "of." The question asks for the percent, so that will be x, the unknown. The following equation is set up:

$$\frac{20}{100} = \frac{x}{100}$$

Cross-multiplying yields the equation 100x = 20(100). Solving for x gives the answer of 20%.

<u>Example 3</u>
30% of what number is 30?

The following equation uses the clues and numbers in the problem:

$$\frac{30}{x} = \frac{30}{100}$$

Cross-multiplying results in the equation 30(100) = 30x. Solving for x gives the answer x = 100.

Problems Involving Estimation

Sometimes when multiplying numbers, the result can be estimated by *rounding*. For example, to estimate the value of 11.2×2.01, each number can be rounded to the nearest integer. This will yield a result of 22.

Rate, Percent, and Measurement Problems

A *ratio* compares the size of one group to the size of another. For example, there may be a room with 4 tables and 24 chairs. The ratio of tables to chairs is 4: 24. Such ratios behave like fractions in that both sides of the ratio by the same number can be multiplied or divided. Thus, the ratio 4:24 is the same as the ratio 2:12 and 1:6.

One quantity is *proportional* to another quantity if the first quantity is always some multiple of the second. For instance, the distance travelled in five hours is always five times to the speed as travelled. The distance is proportional to speed in this case.

One quantity is *inversely proportional* to another quantity if the first quantity is equal to some number divided by the second quantity. The time it takes to travel one hundred miles will be given by 100 divided by the speed travelled. The time is inversely proportional to the speed.

When dealing with word problems, there is no fixed series of steps to follow, but there are some general guidelines to use. It is important that the quantity that to be found is identified. Then, it can be determined how the given values can be used and manipulated to find the final answer.

Example 1

Jana wants to travel to visit Alice, who lives one hundred and fifty miles away. If she can drive at fifty miles per hour, how long will her trip take?

The quantity to find is the *time* of the trip. The time of a trip is given by the distance to travel divided by the speed to be traveled. The problem determines that the distance is one hundred and fifty miles, while the speed is fifty miles per hour. Thus, 150 divided by 50 is $150 \div 50 = 3$. Because *miles* and *miles per hour* are the units being divided, the miles cancel out. The result is 3 hours.

Example 2

Bernard wishes to paint a wall that measures twenty feet wide by eight feet high. It costs ten cents to paint one square foot. How much money will Bernard need for paint?

The final quantity to compute is the *cost* to paint the wall. This will be ten cents ($0.10) for each square foot of area needed to paint. The area to be painted is unknown, but the dimensions of the wall are given; thus, it can be calculated.

The dimensions of the wall are 20 feet wide and 8 feet high. Since the area of a rectangle is length multiplied by width, the area of the wall is 8 x 20 = 160 square feet. Multiplying 0.1 x 160 yields $16 as the cost of the paint.

The *average* or *mean* of a collection of numbers is given by adding those numbers together and then dividing by the total number of values. A *weighted average* or *weighted mean* is given by adding the numbers multiplied by their weights, then dividing by the sum of the weights:

$$\frac{w_1 x_1 + w_2 x_2 + w_3 x_3 \ldots + w_n x_n}{w_1 + w_2 + w_3 + \cdots + w_n}$$

An *ordinary average* is a weighted average where all the weights are 1.

Simple Geometry Problems

There are many key facts related to geometry that are applicable. The sum of the measures of the angles of a triangle are 180°, and for a quadrilateral, the sum is 360°. Rectangles and squares each have four right angles. A *right angle* has a measure of 90°.

Perimeter

The *perimeter* is the distance around a figure or the sum of all sides of a polygon.

The *formula for the perimeter of a square* is four times the length of a side. For example, the following square has side lengths of 5 meters:

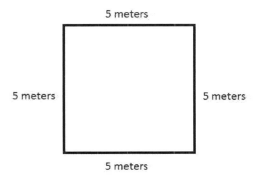

The perimeter is 20 meters because 4 times 5 is 20.

The *formula for a perimeter of a rectangle* is the sum of twice the length and twice the width. For example, if the length of a rectangle is 10 inches and the width 8 inches, then the perimeter is 36 inches because $P = 2l + 2w = 2(10) + 2(8) = 20 + 16 = 36$ inches.

Area

The area is the amount of space inside of a figure, and there are formulas associated with area.

The area of a triangle is the product of one-half the base and height. For example, if the base of the triangle is 2 feet and the height 4 feet, then the area is 4 square feet. The following equation shows the formula used to calculate the area of the triangle:

$$A = \frac{1}{2}bh = \frac{1}{2}(2)(4) = 4 \text{ square feet}$$

The area of a square is the length of a side squared, and the area of a rectangle is length multiplied by the width. For example, if the length of the square is 7 centimeters, then the area is 49 square centimeters. The formula for this example is $A = s^2 = 7^2 = 49$ square centimeters. An example of a rectangle is if the rectangle has a length of 6 inches and a width of 7 inches, then the area is 42 square inches:

$$A = lw = 6(7) = 42 \text{ square inches}$$

The area of a trapezoid is one-half the height times the sum of the bases. For example, if the length of the bases are 2.5 and 3 feet and the height 3.5 feet, then the area is 9.625 square feet. The following formula shows how the area is calculated:

$$A = \frac{1}{2}h(b_1 + b_2) = \frac{1}{2}(3.5)(2.5 + 3) = \frac{1}{2}(3.5)(5.5) = 9.625 \text{ square feet}$$

The perimeter of a figure is measured in single units, while the area is measured in square units.

Distribution of a Quantity into its Fractional Parts

A quantity may be broken into its fractional parts. For example, a toy box holds three types of toys for kids. $\frac{1}{3}$ of the toys are Type A and $\frac{1}{4}$ of the toys are Type B. With that information, how many Type C toys are there?

First, the sum of Type A and Type B must be determined by finding a common denominator to add the fractions. The lowest common multiple is 12, so that is what will be used. The sum is $\frac{1}{3} + \frac{1}{4} = \frac{4}{12} + \frac{3}{12} = \frac{7}{12}$.

This value is subtracted from 1 to find the number of Type C toys. The value is subtracted from 1 because 1 represents a whole. The calculation is $1 - \frac{7}{12} = \frac{12}{12} - \frac{7}{12} = \frac{5}{12}$. This means that $\frac{5}{12}$ of the toys are Type C. To check the answer, add all fractions together, and the result should be 1.

Practice Questions

1. 3.4+2.35+4=
    a. 5.35
    b. 9.2
    c. 9.75
    d. 10.25

2. $5.88 \times 3.2 =$
    a. 18.816
    b. 16.44
    c. 20.352
    d. 17

3. $\frac{3}{25} =$
    a. 0.15
    b. 0.1
    c. 0.9
    d. 0.12

4. Which of the following is largest?
    a. 0.45
    b. 0.096
    c. 0.3
    d. 0.313

5. Which of the following is NOT a way to write 40 percent of N?
    a. $(0.4)N$
    b. $\frac{2}{5}N$
    c. $40N$
    d. $\frac{4N}{10}$

6. Which is closest to 17.8×9.9?
    a. 140
    b. 180
    c. 200
    d. 350

7. A student gets an 85% on a test with 20 questions. How many answers did the student solve correctly?
    a. 15
    b. 16
    c. 17
    d. 18

8. Four people split a bill. The first person pays for $\frac{1}{5}$, the second person pays for $\frac{1}{4}$, and the third person pays for $\frac{1}{3}$. What fraction of the bill does the fourth person pay?

    a. $\frac{13}{60}$

    b. $\frac{47}{60}$

    c. $\frac{1}{4}$

    d. $\frac{4}{15}$

9. 6 is 30% of what number?

    a. 18

    b. 20

    c. 24

    d. 26

10. $3\frac{2}{3} - 1\frac{4}{5} =$

    a. $1\frac{13}{15}$

    b. $\frac{14}{15}$

    c. $2\frac{2}{3}$

    d. $\frac{4}{5}$

11. What is $\frac{420}{98}$ rounded to the nearest integer?

    a. 4

    b. 3

    c. 5

    d. 6

12. $4\frac{1}{3} + 3\frac{3}{4} =$

    a. $6\frac{5}{12}$

    b. $8\frac{1}{12}$

    c. $8\frac{2}{3}$

    d. $7\frac{7}{12}$

13. Five of six numbers have a sum of 25. The average of all six numbers is 6. What is the sixth number?

    a. 8

    b. 10

    c. 11

    d. 12

14. $52.3 \times 10^{-3} =$

    a. 0.00523

    b. 0.0523

    c. 0.523

    d. 523

15. If $\frac{5}{2} \div \frac{1}{3} = n$, then n is between:

    a. 5 and 7

    b. 7 and 9

    c. 9 and 11

    d. 3 and 5

16. A closet is filled with red, blue, and green shirts. If $\frac{1}{3}$ of the shirts are green and $\frac{2}{5}$ are red, what fraction of the shirts are blue?

    a. $\frac{4}{15}$

    b. $\frac{1}{5}$

    c. $\frac{7}{15}$

    d. $\frac{1}{2}$

17. Shawna buys $2\frac{1}{2}$ gallons of paint. If she uses $\frac{1}{3}$ of it on the first day, how much does she have left?

    a. $1\frac{5}{6}$ gallons

    b. $1\frac{1}{2}$ gallons

    c. $1\frac{2}{3}$ gallons

    d. 2 gallons

Answer Explanations

1. C: The decimal points are lined up, with zeroes put in as needed. Then, the numbers are added just like integers:

$$\begin{array}{r} 3.40 \\ 2.35 \\ +4.00 \\ \hline 9.75 \end{array}$$

2. A: This problem can be multiplied as 588×32, except at the end, the decimal point needs to be moved three places to the left. Performing the multiplication will give 18,816, and moving the decimal place over three places results in 18.816.

3. D: The fraction is converted so that the denominator is 100 by multiplying the numerator and denominator by 4, to get $\frac{3}{25} = \frac{12}{100}$. Dividing a number by 100 just moves the decimal point two places to the left, with a result of 0.12.

4. A: Figure out which is largest by looking at the first non-zero digits. Choice B's first non-zero digit is in the hundredths place. The other three all have non-zero digits in the tenths place, so it must be A, C, or D. Of these, A has the largest first non-zero digit.

5. C: $40N$ would be 4000% of N. It's possible to check that each of the others is actually 40% of N.

6. B: Instead of multiplying these out, the product can be estimated by using $18 \times 10 = 180$. The error here should be lower than 15, since it is rounded to the nearest integer, and the numbers add to something less than 30.

7. C: 85% of a number means multiplying that number by 0.85. So, $0.85 \times 20 = \frac{85}{100} \times \frac{20}{1}$, which can be simplified to $\frac{17}{20} \times \frac{20}{1} = 17$.

8. A: To find the fraction of the bill that the first three people pay, the fractions need to be added, which means finding common denominator. The common denominator will be 60. $\frac{1}{5} + \frac{1}{4} + \frac{1}{3} = \frac{12}{60} + \frac{15}{60} + \frac{20}{60} = \frac{47}{60}$. The remainder of the bill is $1 - \frac{47}{60} = \frac{60}{60} - \frac{47}{60} = \frac{13}{60}$.

9. B: 30% is 3/10. The number itself must be 10/3 of 6, or $\frac{10}{3} \times 6 = 10 \times 2 = 20$.

10. A: These numbers to improper fractions: $\frac{11}{3} - \frac{9}{5}$. Take 15 as a common denominator: $\frac{11}{3} - \frac{9}{5} =: \frac{55}{15} - \frac{27}{15} = \frac{28}{15} = 1\frac{13}{15}$ (when rewritten to get rid of the partial fraction).

11. B: Dividing by 98 can be approximated by dividing by 100, which would mean shifting the decimal point of the numerator to the left by 2. The result is 4.2 and rounds to 3.

12. B: $4\frac{1}{3} + 3\frac{3}{4} = 4 + 3 + \frac{1}{3} + \frac{3}{4} = 7 + \frac{1}{3} + \frac{3}{4}$. Adding the fractions gives $\frac{1}{3} + \frac{3}{4} = \frac{4}{12} + \frac{9}{12} = \frac{13}{12} = 1 + \frac{1}{12}$. Thus, $7 + \frac{1}{3} + \frac{3}{4} = 7 + 1 + \frac{1}{12} = 8\frac{1}{12}$.

13. C: The average is calculated by adding all six numbers, then dividing by 6. The first five numbers have a sum of 25. If the total divided by 6 is equal to 6, then the total itself must be 36. The sixth number must be $36 - 25 = 11$.

14. B: Multiplying by 10^{-3} means moving the decimal point three places to the left, putting in zeroes as necessary.

15. B: $\frac{5}{2} \div \frac{1}{3} = \frac{5}{2} \times \frac{3}{1} = \frac{15}{2} = 7.5$.

16. A: The total fraction taken up by green and red shirts will be $\frac{1}{3} + \frac{2}{5} = \frac{5}{15} + \frac{6}{15} = \frac{11}{15}$. The remaining fraction is $1 - \frac{11}{15} = \frac{15}{15} - \frac{11}{15} = \frac{4}{15}$.

17. C: If she has used 1/3 of the paint, she has 2/3 remaining. $2\frac{1}{2}$ gallons are the same as $\frac{5}{2}$ gallons. The calculation is $\frac{2}{3} \times \frac{5}{2} = \frac{5}{3} = 1\frac{2}{3}$ gallons.

College-Level Math

Simplifying Rational Algebraic Expressions

A *rational expression* is a ratio or fraction of two polynomials. An expression is in *lowest terms* when the numerator and denominator have no common factors. The rational expression $\frac{7}{4x+3}$ is in lowest terms because there are no common factors between the numerator and denominator. The rational expression $\frac{x^2+2x+1}{x^2-1}$ can be simplified to $\frac{(x+1)(x+1)}{(x-1)(x+1)} = \frac{x+1}{x-1}$ because there is a common factor of $x+1$.

Factoring

Factors for polynomials are similar to factors for integers—they are numbers, variables, or polynomials that, when multiplied together, give a product equal to the polynomial in question. One polynomial is a factor of a second polynomial if the second polynomial can be obtained from the first by multiplying by a third polynomial.

$6x^6 + 13x^4 + 6x^2$ can be obtained by multiplying together $(3x^4 + 2x^2)(2x^2 + 3)$. This means $2x^2 + 3$ and $3x^4 + 2x^2$ are factors of $6x^6 + 13x^4 + 6x^2$.

In general, finding the factors of a polynomial can be tricky. However, there are a few types of polynomials that can be factored in a straightforward way.

If a certain monomial divides each term of a polynomial, it can be factored out:

$$x^2 + 2xy + y^2 = (x + y)^2$$

$$x^2 - 2xy + y^2 = (x - y)^2$$

$$x^2 - y^2 = (x + y)(x - y)$$

$$x^3 + y^3 = (x + y)(x^2 - xy + y^2)$$

$$x^3 - y^3 = (x - y)(x^2 + xy + y^2)$$

$$x^3 + 3x^2y + 3xy^2 + y^3 = (x + y)^3$$

$$x^3 - 3x^2y + 3xy^2 - y^3 = (x - y)^3$$

These rules can be used in many combinations with one another. For example, the expression $3x^3 - 24$ factors to $3(x^3 - 8) = 3(x - 2)(x^2 + 2x + 4)$.

When factoring polynomials, a good strategy is to multiply the factors to check the result.

Expanding Polynomials

Some polynomials may need to be expanded to identify the final solution—*polynomial expansion* means that parenthetical polynomials are multiplied out so that the parentheses no longer exist. The polynomials will be in the form $(a + b)^n$ where n is a whole number greater than 2. The expression can be simplified using the *distributive property*, which states that a number, variable, or polynomial that is multiplied by a polynomial in parentheses should be multiplied by each item in the parenthetical polynomial. Here's one example:

$$(a + b)^2 = (a + b)(a + b) = a^2 + ab + ab + b^2 = a^2 + 2ab + b^2$$

Here's another example to consider:

$$(a + b)^3 = (a + b)(a + b)(a + b) = (a^2 + ab + ab + b^2)(a + b) = (a^2 + 2ab + b^2)(a + b)$$
$$= a^3 + 2a^2b + ab^2 + a^2b + 2ab^2 + b^3 = a^3 + 3a^2b + 3ab^2 + b^3$$

Manipulating Roots and Exponents

A *root* is a different way to write an exponent when the exponent is the reciprocal of a whole number. We use the *radical* symbol to write this in the following way: $\sqrt[n]{a} = a^{\frac{1}{n}}$. This quantity is called the *n-th root* of *a*. The *n* is called the *index* of the radical.

Note that if the *n-th* root of *a* is multiplied by itself *n* times, the result will just be *a*. If no number *n* is written by the radical, it is assumed that *n* is 2: $\sqrt{5} = 5^{\frac{1}{2}}$. The special case of the 2nd root is called the *square root*, and the third root is called the *cube root*.

A *perfect square* is a whole number that is the square of another whole number. For example, sixteen and 64 are perfect squares because 16 is the square of 4, and 64 is the square of 8.

Solving Linear and Quadratic Equations and Inequalities

An *equation* is an expression that uses an equals sign to demonstrate that two quantities are equal to one another, such as the expression $x^2 - x = -4x + 3$. *Solving* an equation means to find all possible values that *x* can take which make the equation true.

Given an equation where one side is a polynomial in the variable *x* and the other side is zero, the solutions are also called the *roots* or *zeros* of the equation.

To solve an equation, the equation needs to be modified to determine the solution. Starting with an equation $a = b$, the following are also true equations:

$$a + c = b + c$$

$$a - c = b - c$$

$$ac = bc$$

$$a/c = b/c \text{ (provided that } c \text{ is not 0)}$$

$$a^c = b^c$$

$$\sqrt{a} = \pm\sqrt{b}$$

The following rule is important to remember when solving equations:

$$\text{If } ab = 0, \text{ then } a = 0 \text{ or } b = 0.$$

Sometimes, instead of an equation, an *inequality* is used to indicate that one quantity is less than another (or greater than another). They may specify that the two quantities might also be equal to each other. If the quantities are not allowed to equal one another, the expression is a *strict inequality*. For example, $x + 3 \leq 5$ is an inequality, while $7 - 2x > 1$ is a strict inequality.

A *solution set* is a collection of all values of a variable that solve an equation or an inequality. For inequalities, this can be illustrated on a number line by shading in the part of the number line that satisfies the inequality. An open circle on the number line indicates that one gets arbitrarily close to that point, but cannot actually touch that point while remaining in the solution set. For example, to graph the solution set for the inequality $x > 2$, it would look like the following:

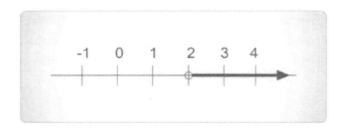

Solution Set x>2

Equation Systems

Sometimes, a problem involves multiple variables and multiple equations that must all hold true at the same time. There are a few basic rules to keep in mind when solving systems of equations.

A single equation can be changed by doing the same operation to both sides, just as with one equation.

If one of the equations gives an expression for one of the variables in terms of other variables and constants, the expression can be substituted into the other equation, in place of the variable. This means the other equations will have one less variable in them.

If two equations are in the form of $a = b$ *and* $c = d$, then a new equation can be formed by adding the equations together, $a + c = b + d$, or subtracting the equations, $a - c = b - d$. This can eliminate one of the variables from an equation.

The general approach is to find a way to change one of the equations so that one variable is isolated, and then substitute that value (or expression) for the variable into the other equations.

The simplest case is a *linear system of two equations*, which has the form $ax + by = c, dx + ey = f$.

To solve linear systems of equations, use the same process to solve one equation in order to isolate one of the variables. Here's an example, using the linear system of equations:

$$2x - 3y = 2, 4x + 4y = 3$$

The first equation is multiplied on both sides by -2, which gives $-4x + 6y = -4$.

Adding this equation to the second equation will allow cancellation of the *x* term: $4x + 4y - 4x + 6y = 3 - 4$.

The result can be simplified to get $10y = -1$, which simplifies to $y = -\frac{1}{10}$.

The solution can be substituted into either of the original equations to find a value for x. Using the first equation, $2x - 3\left(-\frac{1}{10}\right) = 2$.

This simplifies to $2x + \frac{3}{10} = 2$, then to $2x = \frac{17}{10}$, and finally $x = \frac{17}{20}$.

The final solution is $x = \frac{17}{20}, y = -\frac{1}{10}$.

To check the validity of the answer, both solutions can be substituted into either original equation, which should result in a true statement.

An alternative way to solve this system would be to solve the first equation to get an expression for y in terms of x.

Subtracting $2x$ from both sides results in $-3y = 2 - 2x$.

Dividing both sides by -3 would be $y = \frac{2}{3}x - \frac{2}{3}$.

Then, this expression can be substituted into the second equation, getting $4x + 4\left(\frac{2}{3}x - \frac{2}{3}\right) = 3$.

This only involves the variable x, which can now be solved. Once the value for x is obtained, it can be substituted into either equation to solve for y.

There is one important issue to note here. If one of the equations in the system can be made to look identical to another equation, then it is *redundant*. The set of solutions will then be all pairs that satisfy the other equation.

For instance, in the system of equations, $2x - y = 1, -4x + 2y = -2$, the second equation can be made into the first equation by dividing both sides by -2. Thus, the solution set will be all pairs satisfying $2x - y = 1$, which simplifies to $y = 2x - 1$.

For a pair of linear equations, the simplest way to see if one equation is redundant is to rewrite each equation to the form $ax + by = c$. If one equation can be obtained from the other in this form by multiplying both sides by some constant, then the equations are redundant, and the answer to the system would be all real numbers.

It is also possible for the two equations to be *inconsistent*, which occurs when the two equations can be made into the form $ax + by = c, ax + by = d$, with c and d being different numbers. The two equations are inconsistent if, while trying to solve them, it is determined that an equation is false, such as $3 = 2$. This result shows that there are no solutions to that system of equations.

For linear systems of two equations with two variables, there will always be a single solution unless one of the two equations is redundant or the equations are inconsistent, in which case there are no solutions.

Other Algebraic Functions

A *function* $f(x)$ is a mathematical object which takes one number, x, as an input and gives a number in return. The input is called the *independent variable*. If the variable is set equal to the output, as in $y = f(x)$, then this is called the *dependent variable*. To indicate the dependent value a function, y, gives for a specific independent variable, x, the notation $y = f(x)$ is used.

The *domain* of a function is the set of values that the independent variable is allowed to take. Unless otherwise specified, the domain is any value for which the function is well defined. The *range* of the function is the set of possible outputs for the function.

In many cases, a function can be defined by giving an equation. For instance, $f(x) = x^2$ indicates that given a value for x, the output of f is found by squaring x.

Not all equations in x and y can be written in the form $y = f(x)$. An equation can be written in such a form if it satisfies the *vertical line test*: no vertical line meets the graph of the equation at more than a single point. In this case, y is said to be a *function of x*. If a vertical line meets the graph in two places, then this equation cannot be written in the form $y = f(x)$.

The graph of a function $f(x)$ is the graph of the equation $y = f(x)$. Thus, it is the set of all pairs (x, y) where $y = f(x)$. In other words, it is all pairs $(x, f(x))$. The x-intercepts are called the *zeros* of the function. The y-intercept is given by $f(0)$.

If, for a given function f, the only way to get $f(a) = f(b)$ is for $a = b$, then f is *one-to-one*. Often, even if a function is not one-to-one on its entire domain, it is one-to-one by considering a restricted portion of the domain.

A function $f(x) = k$ for some number k is called a *constant function*. The graph of a constant function is a horizontal line.

The function $f(x) = x$ is called the *identity function*. The graph of the identity function is the diagonal line pointing to the upper right at 45 degrees, $y = x$.

Given two functions, $f(x)$ *and* $g(x)$, new functions can be formed by adding, subtracting, multiplying, or dividing the functions. Any algebraic combination of the two functions can be performed, including one function being the exponent of the other. If there are expressions for f and g, then the result can be found by performing the desired operation between the expressions. So, if $f(x) = x^2$ and $g(x) = 3x$, then $f \cdot g(x) = x^2 \cdot 3x = 3x^3$.

Given two functions, $f(x)$ *and* $g(x)$, where the domain of g contains the range of f, the two functions can be combined together in a process called *composition*. The function—"g composed of f"—is written $(g \circ f)(x) = g(f(x))$. This requires the input of x into f, then taking that result and plugging it in to the function g.

If f is one-to-one, then there is also the option to find the function $f^{-1}(x)$, called the *inverse* of f. Algebraically, the inverse function can be found by writing y in place of $f(x)$, and then solving for x. The inverse function also makes this statement true: $f^{-1}(f(x)) = x$.

Computing the inverse of a function f entails the following procedure:

Given $f(x) = x^2$, with a domain of $x \geq 0$

$x = y^2$ is written down o find the inverse

The square root of both sides is determined to solve for y

Normally, this would mean $\pm\sqrt{x} = y$. However, the domain of f does not include the negative numbers, so the negative option needs to be eliminated.

The result is $y = \sqrt{x}$, so $f^{-1}(x) = \sqrt{x}$, with a domain of $x \geq 0$.

A function is called *monotone* if it is either always increasing or always decreasing. For example, the functions $f(x) = 3x$ and $f(x) = -x^5$ are monotone.

An *even function* looks the same when flipped over the y-axis: $f(x) = f(-x)$. The following image shows a graphic representation of an even function.

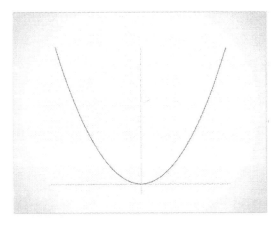

An *odd function* looks the same when flipped over the y-axis and then flipped over the x-axis: $f(x) = -f(-x)$. The following image shows an example of an odd function.

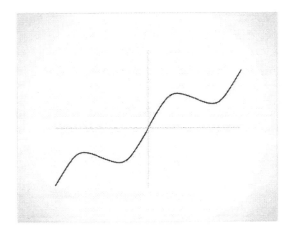

Plane Geometry

Algebraic equations can be used to describe geometric figures in the plane. The method for doing so is to use the *Cartesian coordinate plane*. The idea behind these Cartesian coordinates (named for mathematician and philosopher Descartes) is that from a specific point on the plane, known as the *center*, one can specify any other point by saying *how far to the right or left* and *how far up or down*.

The plane is covered with a grid. The two directions, right to left and bottom to top, are called *axes* (singular *axis*). When working with x and y variables, the x variable corresponds to the right and left axis, and the y variable corresponds to the up and down axis.

Any point on the grid is found by specifying how far to travel from the center along the x-axis and how far to travel along the y-axis. The ordered pair can be written as (x, y). A positive x value means go to the right on the x-axis, while a negative x value means to go to the left. A positive y value means to go up, while a negative value means to go down. Several points are shown as examples in the figure.

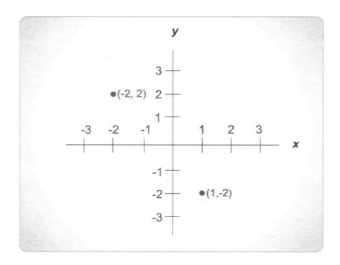

Cartesian Coordinate Plane

The Coordinate Plane

The coordinate plane can be divided into four *quadrants*. The upper-right part of the plane is called the *first quadrant*, where both x and y are positive. The *second quadrant* is the upper-left, where x is negative but y is positive. The *third quadrant* is the lower left, where both x and y are negative. Finally, the *fourth quadrant* is in the lower right, where x is positive but y is negative. These quadrants are often written with Roman numerals:

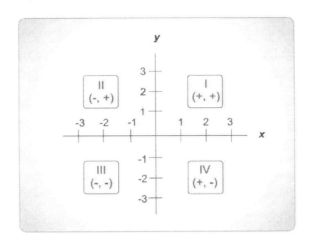

In addition to graphing individual points as shown above, the graph lines and curves in the plane can be graphed corresponding to equations. In general, if there is some equation involving x and y, then the *graph* of that equation consists of all the points (x, y) in the Cartesian coordinate plane, which satisfy this equation.

Given the equation $y = x + 2$, the point $(0, 2)$ is in the graph, since $2 = 0 + 2$ is a true equation. However, the point $(1, 4)$ will *not* be in the graph, because $4 = 1 + 2$ is false.

Straight Lines

The simplest equations to graph are the equations whose graphs are lines, called *linear equations*. Every linear equation can be rewritten algebraically so that it looks like $Ax + By = C$.

First, the ratio of the change in the y coordinate to the change in the x coordinate is constant for any two distinct points on the line. In any pair of points on a line, two points, (x_1, y_1) and (x_2, y_2)—

where $x_1 \neq x_2$—the ratio $\frac{y_2 - y_1}{x_2 - x_1}$ will always be the same, even if another pair of points is used.

This ratio, $\frac{y_2 - y_1}{x_2 - x_1}$, is called the *slope* of the line and is often denoted with the letter m. If the slope is *positive*, then the line goes upward when moving to the right. If the slope is *negative*, then it moves downward when moving to the right. If the slope is 0, then the line is *horizontal*, and the y coordinate is constant along the entire line. For lines where the x coordinate is constant along the entire line, the slope is not defined, and these lines are called *vertical* lines.

The y coordinate of the point where the line touches the y-axis is called the *y-intercept* of the line. It is often denoted by the letter b, used in the form of the linear equation $y = mx + b$. The x coordinate of the point where the line touches the x-axis is called the *x-intercept*. It is also called the *zero* of the line.

Suppose two lines have slopes m_1 and m_2. If the slopes are equal, $m_1 = m_2$, then the lines are *parallel*. Parallel lines never meet one another. If $m_1 = -\frac{1}{m_2}$, then the lines are called *perpendicular* or *orthogonal*. Their slopes can also be called opposite reciprocals of each other.

There are several convenient ways to write down linear equations. The common forms are listed here:

Standard Form: $Ax + By = C$, where the slope is given by $\frac{-A}{B}$, and the *y*-intercept is given by $\frac{C}{B}$.

Slope-Intercept Form: $y = mx + b$, where the slope is *m*, and the *y*-intercept is *b*.

Point-Slope Form: $y - y_1 = m(x - x_1)$, where *m* is the slope, and (x_1, y_1) is any point on the line.

Two-Point Form: $\frac{y-y_1}{x-x_1} = \frac{y_2-y_1}{x_2-x_1}$, where (x_1, y_1), and (x_2, y_2) are any two distinct points on the line.

Intercept Form: $\frac{x}{x_1} + \frac{y}{y_1} = 1$, where x_1 is the *x*-intercept, and y_1 is the *y*-intercept.

Depending upon the given information, different forms of the linear equation can be easier to write down than others. When given two points, the two-point form is easy to write down. If the slope and a single point is known, the point-slope form is easiest to start with. In general, which form to start with depends upon the given information.

Conics

The graph of an equation of the form $y = ax^2 + bx + c$ or $x = ay^2 + by + c$ is called a *parabola*.

The graph of an equation of the form $\frac{x^2}{a^2} - \frac{y^2}{b^2} = 1$ or $-\frac{x^2}{a^2} + \frac{y^2}{b^2} = 1$ is called a *hyperbola*.

The graph of an equation of the form $\frac{(x-x_0)^2}{a^2} + \frac{(y-y_0)^2}{b^2} = 1$ is called an *ellipse*. If $a = b$ then this is a circle with *radius* $r = \frac{1}{a}$.

Sets of Points in the Plane

The *midpoint* between two points, (x_1, y_1) and (x_2, y_2), is given by taking the average of the *x* coordinates and the average of the *y* coordinates: $\left(\frac{x_1+x_2}{2}, \frac{y_1+y_2}{2}\right)$.

The *distance* between two points, (x_1, y_1) and (x_2, y_2), is given by the *Pythagorean formula*, $\sqrt{(x_2 - x_1)^2 + (y_2 - y_1)^2}$.

To find the perpendicular distance between a line $Ax + By = C$ and a point (x_1, y_1) not on the line, we need to use the formula $\frac{|Ax_1+By_1+C|}{\sqrt{A^2+B^2}}$.

Graphs of Algebraic Functions

A graph can shift in many ways. To shift it horizontally, a constant can be added to all the *x* variables. Replacing *x* with $(x + a)$ will shift the graph to the left by *a*. If *a* is negative, this shifts the graph to the right. Similarly, vertical shifts occur by adding a constant to each of the *y* variables. Replacing *y* by $(y + a)$ will shift the graph up by *a*. If *a* is negative, then it shifts the graph down.

A graph can also stretch and shrink the graph in the horizontal and vertical directions. To stretch by a (positive) factor of *k* horizontally, all instances of *x* are replaced with $\frac{x}{k}$. To stretch vertically by *k*, all instances of *y* are replaced with $\frac{y}{k}$.

The graph can be reflected over the y-axis by replacing all instances of x with $(-x)$. The graph can also be reflected over the x-axis by replacing all instances of y with $(-y)$.

Complex Numbers

Some types of equations can be solved to find real answers, but this is not the case for all equations. For example, $x^2 = k$ can be solved when k is non-negative, but it has no real solutions when k is negative. Equations do have solutions if complex numbers are allowed.

Complex numbers are defined in the following manner: every complex number can be written as $a + bi$, where $i^2 = -1$. Thus, the solutions to the equation $x^2 = -1$ are $\pm i$.

In order to find roots of negative numbers more generally, the properties of roots (or of exponents) are used. For example, $\sqrt{-4} = \sqrt{-1}\sqrt{4} = \pm 2i$. All arithmetic operations can be performed with complex numbers, where i is like any other constant. The value of i^2 can replace -1.

Series and Sequences

A *sequence* is an infinite, ordered list of numbers and a function whose domain is an infinite subset of non-negative integers. Usually, the domain will be all non-negative integers, or else all positive integers, but sometimes, it is convenient to use a smaller subset for some sequences. Although it would be possible to use function notation, it is customary to write sequences a little bit differently.

Given a sequence defined by some function, the value of this function is written on n as a_n and denoted in the entire sequence as $\{a_n\}$. The sequence can be written $a_1, a_2, a_3, \dots a_n, \dots$, keeping in mind this list continues infinitely. The a_n values are called the *terms* of the sequence.

In some cases, a formula for a_n is an expression that only involves n and constants. In some other cases, an expression for a_n involves only n, constants, and a_{n-1}. This latter case is called a *recursive* definition for the sequences.

An *infinite sum* or simply *sum* of a sequence $\{a_n\}$ is a sequence $\{s_n\}$, where $s_n = a_1 + a_2 + \cdots + a_n$. Some sequences have the property of getting closer to one particular value. The value is the *limit* of the sequence.

If the limit of a sequence $\{a_n\}$ is L, this means that for any positive real number δ, there is a value of M, as long as $n > M$, $|a_n - L| < \delta$. This is just a very formal way of saying that for any real number positive (real number δ), there is a point where all the remaining values are within δ of L in the sequence. This just means, on the whole, getting closer to L as the sequence ends. This is a *limit* of a sequence $\lim_{n\to\infty} a_n$.

If a sequence has a limit, the sequence *converges*. On the other hand, if the absolute value $|a_n|$ keeps on getting bigger, the sequence *diverges*.

Some sequences do not converge or diverge. For example, the sequence $a_n = \begin{cases} 1, n \text{ odd} \\ -1, n \text{ even} \end{cases}$, flips back and forth between 1 and -1. This sequence never converges, since it keeps bouncing back and forth. However, it does not diverge, either, since the absolute value is never bigger than 1.

In order to find the limit of a sequence, we can use the following rules:

- $\lim_{n\to\infty} k = k$ for all real numbers k.

- $\lim_{n\to\infty} \frac{1}{n} = 0$.

- $\lim_{n\to\infty} n = \infty$.

- $\lim_{n\to\infty} \frac{k}{n^p} = 0$ when k is real and p is a positive rational number.

- $\lim_{n\to\infty}(a_n + b_n) = \lim_{n\to\infty} a_n + \lim_{n\to\infty} b_n$

- $\lim_{n\to\infty}(a_n - b_n) = \lim_{n\to\infty} a_n - \lim_{n\to\infty} b_n$

- $\lim_{n\to\infty}(a_n \cdot b_n) = \lim_{n\to\infty} a_n \cdot \lim_{n\to\infty} b_n$. As a special case, $\lim_{n\to\infty} ka_n = k \lim_{n\to\infty} a_n$

- $\lim_{n\to\infty}\left(\frac{a_n}{b_n}\right) = \frac{\lim_{n\to\infty} a_n}{\lim_{n\to\infty} b_n}$ when $\lim_{n\to\infty} b_n$ is not 0.

A sequence is called *monotonic* if the terms of the sequence never decrease or if they never increase. In other words, $\{a_n\}$ is monotonic if one of two things happen: either $a_n \geq a_m$ whenever $n > m$ (in this case, the sequences is also called *non-decreasing*), or else $a_n \leq a_m$ whenever $n > m$ (in this case, the sequence is also called *non-increasing*).

A sequence is said to be *bounded above* by k if, for any value of n, every $a_n \leq k$, and *bounded below* by k if $a_n \geq k$. Every non-decreasing sequence that is bounded above converges to some real number. Every non-increasing sequence that is bounded below converges to some real number.

An *arithmetic sequence* is a sequence where the next term is obtained from the previous term by adding a specific quantity, k. In other words, $a_{n+1} = a_n + k$. Another way of writing this out is the sequence $a_1, a_1 + k, a_1 + 2k, \dots, a_1 + (n-1)k \dots$. That is, $a_n = a_1 + (n-1)k$. The *sum* of the first n terms of an arithmetic sequence is $s_n = \frac{n}{2}(a_1 + a_n)$.

A *geometric sequence* (or a *geometric progression*) is a sequence in which for some specific quantity r, $a_{n+1} = ra_n$. Another way of writing this is that the sequence is $a_1, a_1 r, a_1 r^2, \dots, a_1 r^{n-1} \dots$. The general formula is $a_n = a_1 r^{n-1}$. The sum of the first n terms of a geometric sequence is $s_n = \frac{a_1(1-r^n)}{1-r}$.

A *series* or *infinite series* is a sequence $\{s_n\}$, whose n-th term is the sum of the first n terms of some sequence $\{a_n\}$. Thus, $s_n = a_1 + a_2 + \cdots + a_n$ can also be written as $\sum_{m=1}^{n} a_m$.

Each s_n is the sum of the first n terms and is called the *n-th partial sum*. The *infinite sum* (or simply, *sum*) of a sequence $\{a_n\}$ is the limit of the sequence $\{s_n\}$, also written as $\sum_{n=1}^{\infty} a_n$.

A series can converge, diverge, or neither, just like a sequence. The rules for finding whether or not a series converges or diverges are identical to the rules for sequences. When a series is being added or subtracted, or multiplied by constants, it obeys the following rules:

$$\sum_{n=1}^{\infty}(a_n + b_n) = \sum_{n=1}^{\infty} a_n + \sum_{n=1}^{\infty} b_n$$

$$\sum_{n=1}^{\infty} (a_n - b_n) = \sum_{n=1}^{\infty} a_n - \sum_{n=1}^{\infty} b_n$$

$$\sum_{n=1}^{\infty} k a_n = k \sum_{n=1}^{\infty} a_n$$

A *geometric series* is a sum of a geometric sequence: $\sum_{n=1}^{\infty} ar^{n-1} = a_1 + a_2 r + \cdots + a_n r^{n-1} + \cdots$. In such a series, when $|r| \geq 1$, the series diverges. However, when $|r| < 1$, then $\sum_{n=1}^{\infty} ar^{n-1} = \frac{a}{1-r}$.

It's important to note that whenever a sum $\sum_{n=1}^{\infty} a_n$ converges, the sequence $\{a_n\}$ has a limit of 0: $\lim_{n \to \infty} a_n = 0$. This is one possible test to see whether or not a series converges. However, just because this limit is zero does not mean that the sum diverges, so the test only works in one direction.

Determinants

A *matrix* is a rectangular arrangement of numbers in rows and columns. The *determinant* of a matrix is a special value that can be calculated for any square matrix.

Using the *square 2 x 2 matrix* $\begin{bmatrix} a & b \\ c & d \end{bmatrix}$, the determinant is $ad - bc$.

For example, the determinant of the matrix $\begin{bmatrix} -5 & 1 \\ 3 & 4 \end{bmatrix}$ is *-5(4) – 1(3) = -20 – 3 = -23*.

Using a *3 x 3 matrix* $\begin{bmatrix} a & b & c \\ d & e & f \\ g & h & i \end{bmatrix}$, the determinant is $a(ei - fh) - b(di - fg) + c(dh - eg)$.

For example, the determinant of the matrix $\begin{bmatrix} 2 & 0 & 1 \\ -1 & 3 & 2 \\ 2 & -2 & -1 \end{bmatrix}$ is

$$2\big(3(-1) - 2(-2)\big) - 0\big(-1(-1) - 2(2)\big) + 1\big(-1(-2) - 3(2)\big)$$

$$= 2(-3 + 4) - 0(1 - 4) + 1(2 - 6)$$

$$= 2(1) - 0(-3) + 1(-4)$$

$$= 2 - 0 - 4 = -2$$

The pattern continues for larger square matrices.

Permutations and Combinations

The *factorial* is defined for non-negative integers. The factorial of n is written as $n!$ For positive integers, the factorial is defined as the product of all positive integers up to n. So, $n! = 1 \cdot 2 \cdot \ldots \cdot n$.

For zero, $0! = 1$. The reason for zero being a special case is two-fold. First, the relation is always $n! = n \cdot (n-1)!$ when the right hand side is defined. Second, it makes the choice functions below work out correctly.

The *combinatorial choice function* indicates how many distinct ways one can choose to pick out k objects from a set of n objects. The choice function is written as $\binom{n}{k}$—read as "n choose k"—and is given by $\binom{n}{k} = \frac{n!}{k! \cdot (n-k)!}$.

As an example, suppose a person wanted to choose three shirts out of five shirts to take on a trip. How many ways can this be done?

The answer is given by computing 5 choose 3. $\binom{5}{3} = \frac{5!}{3! \cdot (5-3)!} = \frac{5 \cdot 4 \cdot 3 \cdot 2 \cdot 1}{3 \cdot 2 \cdot 1 \cdot 2 \cdot 1}$. At this stage, all the indicated multiplications can be calculated, but a number of common factors cancel first. (The appearance of many common factors is normal when computing choice functions.)

The expression simplifies to, $\frac{5 \cdot 4 \cdot 3 \cdot 2 \cdot 1}{3 \cdot 2 \cdot 1 \cdot 2 \cdot 1} = \frac{5 \cdot 4}{2 \cdot 1} = \frac{20}{2} = 10$.

There are ten different combinations of three shirts.

Using the choice function, it can be calculated how many ways to order a set of objects. Ordering a set of n objects requires choosing a first object out of n objects, then picking a second object out of the remaining $n - 1$ objects. Then a third object out of the $n - 2$ objects can be picked, and so on. Therefore, the total number of ways to order n objects will be $\binom{n}{1}\binom{n-1}{1} \ldots \binom{1}{1}$

Fractions and Word Problems

Work word problems are examples of people working together in a situation that uses fractions.

Example
One painter can paint a designated room in 6 hours, and a second painter can paint the same room in 5 hours. How long will it take them to paint the room if they work together?

The first painter paints $\frac{1}{6}$ of the room in an hour, and the second painter paints $\frac{1}{5}$ of the room in an hour.

Together, they can paint $\frac{1}{x}$ of the room in an hour. The equation is the sum of the painters rate equal to the total job or $\frac{1}{6} + \frac{1}{5} = \frac{1}{x}$.

The equation can be solved by multiplying all terms by a common denominator of $30x$ with a result of $5x + 6x = 30$.

The left side can be added together to get $11x$, and then divide by 11 for a solution of $\frac{30}{11}$ or about 2.73 hours.

Polynomials

Algebraic expressions are built out of monomials. A *monomial* is a variable raised to some power multiplied by a constant: ax^n, where a is any constant and n is a whole number. A constant is also a monomial.

A *polynomial* is a sum of monomials. Examples of polynomials include $3x^4 + 2x^2 - x - 3$ and $\frac{4}{5}x^3$. The latter is also a monomial. If the highest power of x is 1, the polynomial is called *linear*. If the highest power of x is 2, it is called *quadratic*.

Algebraic

A function is called *algebraic* if it is built up from polynomials by adding, subtracting, multiplying, dividing, and taking radicals. This means that, for example, the variable can never appear in an exponent. Thus, polynomials and rational functions are algebraic, but exponential functions are not algebraic. It turns out that logarithms and trigonometric functions are not algebraic either.

A function of the form $f(x) = a_n x^n + a_{n-1} x^{n-1} + a_{n-2} x^{n-2} + \cdots + a_1 x + a_0$ is called a *polynomial function*. The value of n is called the *degree* of the polynomial. In the case where $n = 1$, it is called a *linear function*. In the case where $n = 2$, it is called a *quadratic function*. In the case where $n = 3$, it is called a *cubic function*.

When n is even, the polynomial is called *even*, and not all real numbers will be in its range. When n is odd, the polynomial is called *odd*, and the range includes all real numbers.

The graph of a quadratic function $f(x) = ax^2 + bx + c$ will be a parabola. To see whether or not the parabola opens up or down, it's necessary to check the coefficient of x^2, which is the value a.

If the coefficient is positive, then the parabola opens upward. If the coefficient is negative, then the parabola opens downward.

The quantity $D = b^2 - 4ac$ is called the *discriminant* of the parabola. If the discriminant is positive, then the parabola has two real zeros. If the discriminant is negative, then it has no real zeros.

If the discriminant is zero, then the parabola's highest or lowest point is on the x-axis, and it has a single real zero.

The highest or lowest point of the parabola is called the *vertex*. The coordinates of the vertex are given by the point $(-\frac{b}{2a}, -\frac{D}{4a})$. The roots of a quadratic function can be found with the quadratic formula, which is $x = \frac{-b \pm \sqrt{b^2 - 4ac}}{2a}$.

A *rational function* is a function $f(x) = \frac{p(x)}{q(x)}$, where p and q are both polynomials. The domain of f will be all real numbers except the (real) roots of q.

At these roots, the graph of f will have a *vertical asymptote*, unless they are also roots of p. Here is an example to consider:

$$p(x) = p_n x^n + p_{n-1} x^{n-1} + p_{n-2} x^{n-2} + \cdots + p_1 x + p_0$$

$$q(x) = q_m x^m + q_{m-1} x^{m-1} + q_{m-2} x^{m-2} + \cdots + q_1 x + q_0$$

When the degree of p is less than the degree of q, there will be a horizontal asymptote of $y = 0$. If p and q have the same degree, there will be a horizontal asymptote of $y = \frac{p_n}{q_n}$. If the degree of p is exactly one greater than the degree of q, then f will have an oblique asymptote along the line $y = \frac{p_n}{q_{n-1}} x + \frac{p_{n-1}}{q_{n-1}}$.

Exponentials

An *exponential function* is a function of the form $f(x) = b^x$, where b is a positive real number other than 1. In such a function, b is called the *base*.

The *domain* of an exponential function is all real numbers, and the *range* is all positive real numbers. There will always be a horizontal asymptote of $y = 0$ on one side. If b is greater than 1, then the graph will be increasing moving to the right. If b is less than 1, then the graph will be decreasing moving to the right. Exponential functions are one-to-one. The basic exponential function graph will go through the point (0,1).

Example
Solve $5^{x+1} = 25$.

Get the x out of the exponent by rewriting the equation $5^{x+1} = 5^2$ so that both sides have a base of 5.

Since the bases are the same, the exponents must be equal to each other.

This leaves $x + 1 = 2$ or $x = 1$.

To check the answer, the x-value of 1 can be substituted back into the original equation.

Logarithmic

A *logarithmic function* is an inverse for an exponential function. The inverse of the base b exponential function is written as $\log_b(x)$, and is called the *base b logarithm*. The domain of a logarithm is all positive real numbers. It has the properties that $\log_b(b^x) = x$. For positive real values of x, $b^{\log_b(x)} = x$.

When there is no chance of confusion, the parentheses are sometimes skipped for logarithmic functions: $\log_b(x)$ may be written as $\log_b x$. For the special number e, the base e logarithm is called the *natural logarithm* and is written as $\ln x$. Logarithms are one-to-one.

When working with logarithmic functions, it is important to remember the following properties. Each one can be derived from the definition of the logarithm as the inverse to an exponential function:

$$\log_b 1 = 0$$

$$\log_b b = 1$$

$$\log_b b^p = p$$

$$\log_b MN = \log_b M + \log_b N$$

$$\log_b \frac{M}{N} = \log_b M - \log_b N$$

$$\log_b M^p = p \log_b M$$

When solving equations involving exponentials and logarithms, the following fact should be used:

If f is a one-to-one function, $a = b$ is equivalent to $f(a) = f(b)$.

Using this, together with the fact that logarithms and exponentials are inverses, allows manipulations of the equations to isolate the variable.

<u>Example</u>
Solve $4 = \ln(x - 4)$.

Using the definition of a logarithm, the equation can be changed to $e^4 = e^{\ln(x-4)}$.

The functions on the right side cancel with a result of $e^4 = x - 4$.

This then gives $x = 4 + e^4$.

Trigonometric Functions

Trigonometric functions are built out of two basic functions, the *sine* and *cosine*, written as $\sin\theta$ and $\cos\theta$ respectively. Note that similar to logarithms, it is customary to drop the parentheses as long as the result is not confusing.

The sine and cosine are defined using the *unit circle*. If θ is the angle going counterclockwise around the origin from the *x*-axis, then the point on the unit circle in that direction will have the coordinates $(\cos\theta, \sin\theta)$.

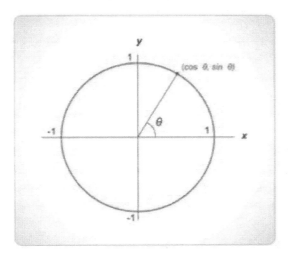

Since the angle returns to the start every 2π radians (or 360 degrees), the graph of these functions will be *periodic*, with period 2π. This means that the graph repeats itself as one moves along the *x*-axis because $\sin\theta = \sin(\theta + 2\pi)$. Cosine is works similarly.

From the unit circle definition, the sine function starts at 0 when $\theta = 0$. It grows to 1 as θ grows to $\pi/2$, and then back to 0 at $\theta = \pi$. Then it decreases to -1 as θ grows to $3\pi/2$, and back up to 0 at $\theta = 2\pi$.

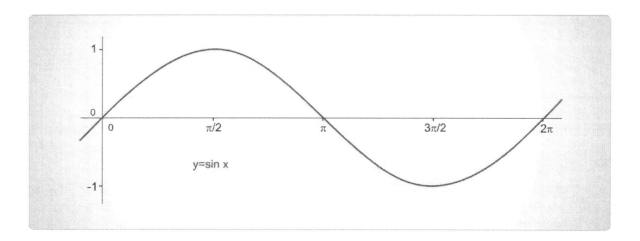

The graph of the cosine is similar. The cosine will start at 1, decreasing to 0 at $\pi/2$ and continuing to decrease to -1 at $\theta = \pi$. Then, it grows to 0 as θ grows to $3\pi/2$ and back up to 1 at $\theta = 2\pi$.

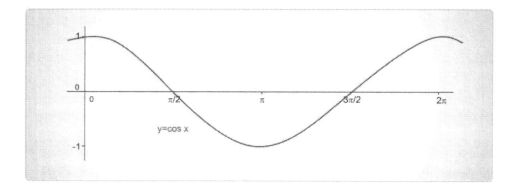

Another trigonometric function, which is frequently used, is the *tangent* function. This is defined as the following equation: $\tan \theta = \frac{\sin \theta}{\cos \theta}$.

The tangent function is a period of π rather than 2π because the sine and cosine functions have the same absolute values after a change in the angle of π, but flip their signs. Since the tangent is a ratio of the two functions, the changes in signs cancel.

The tangent function will be zero when the sine is zero, and it will have a vertical asymptote whenever cosine is zero. The following graph shows the tangent function:

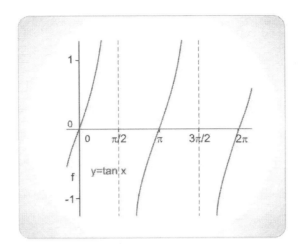

Three other trigonometric functions are sometimes useful. These are the *reciprocal* trigonometric functions, so named because they are just the reciprocals of sine, cosine, and tangent. They are the *cosecant*, defined as $\csc\theta = \frac{1}{\sin\theta}$, the *secant*, $\sec\theta = \frac{1}{\cos\theta}$, and the *cotangent*, $\cot\theta = \frac{1}{\tan\theta}$. Note that from the definition of tangent, $\cot\theta = \frac{\cos\theta}{\sin\theta}$.

In addition, there are three identities that relate the trigonometric functions to one another:

$$\cos\theta = \sin(\frac{\pi}{2} - \theta)$$

$$\csc\theta = \sec\left(\frac{\pi}{2} - \theta\right)$$

$$\cot\theta = \tan(\frac{\pi}{2} - \theta)$$

Here is a list of commonly-needed values for trigonometric functions, given in radians, for the first quadrant:

Table for trigonometric functions

$\sin 0 = 0$	$\cos 0 = 1$	$\tan 0 = 0$
$\sin\dfrac{\pi}{6} = \dfrac{1}{2}$	$\cos\dfrac{\pi}{6} = \dfrac{\sqrt{3}}{2}$	$\tan\dfrac{\pi}{6} = \dfrac{\sqrt{3}}{3}$
$\sin\dfrac{\pi}{4} = \dfrac{\sqrt{2}}{2}$	$\cos\dfrac{\pi}{4} = \dfrac{\sqrt{2}}{2}$	$\tan\dfrac{\pi}{4} = 1$
$\sin\dfrac{\pi}{3} = \dfrac{\sqrt{3}}{2}$	$\cos\dfrac{\pi}{3} = \dfrac{1}{2}$	$\tan\dfrac{\pi}{3} = \sqrt{3}$
$\sin\dfrac{\pi}{2} = 1$	$\cos\dfrac{\pi}{2} = 0$	$\tan\dfrac{\pi}{2} = undefined$
$\csc 0 = undefined$	$\sec 0 = 1$	$\cot 0 = undefined$
$\csc\dfrac{\pi}{6} = 2$	$\sec\dfrac{\pi}{6} = \dfrac{2\sqrt{3}}{3}$	$\cot\dfrac{\pi}{6} = \sqrt{3}$
$\csc\dfrac{\pi}{4} = \sqrt{2}$	$\sec\dfrac{\pi}{4} = \sqrt{2}$	$\cot\dfrac{\pi}{4} = 1$
$\csc\dfrac{\pi}{3} = \dfrac{2\sqrt{3}}{3}$	$\sec\dfrac{\pi}{3} = 2$	$\cot\dfrac{\pi}{3} = \dfrac{\sqrt{3}}{3}$
$\csc\dfrac{\pi}{2} = 1$	$\sec\dfrac{\pi}{2} = undefined$	$\cot\dfrac{\pi}{2} = 0$

To find the trigonometric values in other quadrants, complementary angles can be used. The *complementary angle* is the smallest angle between the *x*-axis and the given angle.

Once the complementary angle is known, the following rule is used:

For an angle θ with complementary angle x, the absolute value of a trigonometry function evaluated at θ is the same as the absolute value when evaluated at x.

The correct sign is used based on the functions sine and cosine are given by the *x* and *y* coordinates on the unit circle.

Sine will be positive in quadrants I and II and negative in quadrants III and IV.

Cosine will be positive in quadrants I and IV, and negative in II and III.

Tangent will be positive in I and III, and negative in II and IV.

The signs of the reciprocal functions will be the same as the sign of the function of which they are a reciprocal.

Example

Find $\sin\frac{3\pi}{4}$.

First, the complementary angle must be found.

This angle is in the II quadrant, and the angle between it and the x-axis is $\frac{\pi}{4}$.

Now, $\sin\frac{\pi}{4} = \frac{\sqrt{2}}{2}$.

Since this is in the II quadrant, sine takes on positive values (the y coordinate is positive in the II quadrant).

Therefore, $\sin\frac{3\pi}{4} = \frac{\sqrt{2}}{2}$.

In addition to the six trigonometric functions defined above, there are inverses for these functions. However, since the trigonometric functions are not one-to-one, one can only construct inverses for them on a restricted domain.

Usually, the domain chosen will be $[0, \pi)$ for cosine and $(-\frac{\pi}{2}, \frac{\pi}{2}]$ for sine. The inverse for tangent can use either of these domains. The inverse functions for the trigonometric functions are also called *arc functions*. In addition to being written with a -1 in the exponent to denote that the function is an inverse, they will sometimes be written with an "a" or "arc" in front of the function name, so $\cos^{-1}\theta = a\cos\theta = \arccos\theta$.

When solving equations that involve trigonometric functions, there are often multiple solutions. For example, $2\sin\theta = \sqrt{2}$ can be simplified to $\sin\theta = \frac{\sqrt{2}}{2}$. This has solutions $\theta = \frac{\pi}{4}, \frac{3\pi}{4}$, but in addition, because of the periodicity, any integer multiple of 2π can also be added to these solutions to find another solution.

The full set of solutions is $\theta = \frac{\pi}{4} + 2\pi k, \frac{3\pi}{4} + 2\pi k$ for all integer values of k. It is very important to remember to find all possible solutions when dealing with equations that involve trigonometric functions.

The name *trigonometric* comes from the fact that these functions play an important role in the geometry of triangles, particularly right triangles.

Consider the right triangle shown in this figure:

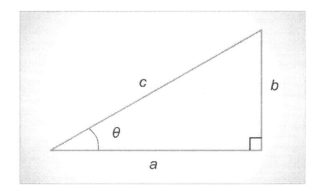

The following hold true:

- $c \sin \theta = b$

- $c \cos \theta = a$

- $\tan \theta = \dfrac{b}{a}$

- $b \csc \theta = c$

- $a \sec \theta = c$

- $\cot \theta = \dfrac{a}{b}$

Remember also the angles of a triangle must add up to π radians (180 degrees).

Practice Questions

1. Find the determinant of the matrix $\begin{bmatrix} -4 & 2 \\ 3 & -1 \end{bmatrix}$.

    a. -10

    b. -2

    c. 0

    d. 2

    e. 10

2. If $a \neq b$, solve for x if $\frac{1}{x} + \frac{2}{a} = \frac{2}{b}$

    a. $\frac{a-b}{ab}$

    b. $\frac{ab}{2(a-b)}$

    c. $\frac{2(a-b)}{ab}$

    d. $\frac{a-b}{2ab}$

    e. $\frac{a^2-b^2}{ab}$

3. If $x^2 + x - 3 = 0$, then $\left(x - \frac{1}{2}\right)^2 =$

    a. $\frac{11}{2}$

    b. $\frac{11}{4}$

    c. 11

    d. $\frac{121}{4}$

    e. 5

4. Which graph will be a line parallel to the graph of $y = 3x - 2$?

    a. $2y - 6x = 2$

    b. $y - 4x = 4$

    c. $3y = x - 2$

    d. $2x - 2y = 2$

    e. $2y = 3x - 2$

5. An equation for the line passing through the origin and the point $(2, 1)$ is

    a. $y = 2x$

    b. $y = \frac{1}{2}x$

    c. $y = x - 2$

    d. $2y = x + 1$

    e. $y = x - 2$

6. Jessica buys 10 cans of paint. Red paint costs $1 per can and blue paint costs $2 per can. In total, she spends $16. How many red cans did she buy?

    a. 2

    b. 3

    c. 4

    d. 5

    e. 6

7. A farmer owns two (non-adjacent) square plots of land, which he wishes to fence. The area of one is 1000 square feet, while the area of the other is 10 square feet. How much fencing does he need, in feet?

    a. 44

    b. $40\sqrt{10}$

    c. $440\sqrt{10}$

    d. $40 + 4\sqrt{10}$

    e. $44\sqrt{10}$

8. If $\log_{10} x = 2$, then x is

    a. 4

    b. 20

    c. 100

    d. 1000

    e. $\sqrt{10}$

9. Let $f(x) = 2x + 1, g(x) = \frac{x-1}{4}$. Find $g(f(x))$.

    a. $\frac{x+1}{2}$

    b. $\frac{x}{2}$

    c. $\frac{2x^2-x-1}{4}$

    d. $3x$

    e. $\frac{x}{4} + 1$

10. Suppose θ is an acute angle, and $\sin \theta = \frac{\sqrt{3}}{2}$. What is $\cos \theta$?

    a. $\frac{1}{2}$

    b. $\frac{\sqrt{3}}{2}$

    c. $\frac{\sqrt{2}}{2}$

    d. $\frac{1}{4}$

    e. Undefined

11. $2x(3x + 1) - 5(3x + 1) =$

    a. $10x(3x + 1)$

    b. $10x^2(3x + 1)$

    c. $(2x - 5)(3x + 1)$

    d. $(2x + 1)(3x - 5)$

    e. $6x^2 - 5$

12. For which real numbers x is $-3x^2 + x - 8 > 0$?

    a. All real numbers x

    b. $-2\sqrt{\frac{2}{3}} < x < 2\sqrt{\frac{2}{3}}$

    c. $1 - 2\sqrt{\frac{2}{3}} < x < 1 + 2\sqrt{\frac{2}{3}}$

    d. $1 < x < 3$

    e. For no real numbers x

13. A root of $x^2 - 2x - 2$ is

    a. $1 + \sqrt{3}$

    b. $1 + 2\sqrt{2}$

    c. $2 + 2\sqrt{3}$

    d. $2 - 2\sqrt{3}$

    e. 3

14. In the xy-plane, the graph of $y = x^2 + 2$ and the circle with center $(0,1)$ and radius 1 have how many points of intersection?

    a. 0

    b. 1

    c. 2

    d. 3

    e. 4

15. A line goes through the point (-4, 0) and the point (0,2). What is the slope of the line?

    a. 2

    b. 4

    c. $\frac{3}{2}$

    d. $\frac{1}{2}$

    e. $\frac{3}{4}$

16. How many different ways can we order the letters a, b, c?

    a. 3

    b. 6

    c. 9

    d. 12

    e. 36

17. If $f(x) = 4x + 2$, and $f^{-1}(x)$ is the inverse function for f, then what is $f^{-1}(6)$?

    a. 0

    b. $\dfrac{1}{2}$

    c. 1

    d. $\dfrac{3}{2}$

    e. 2

18. The sequence $\{a_n\}$ is defined by the relation $a_{n+1} = 3a_n - 1, a_1 = 1$. Find a_3.

    a. 2

    b. 4

    c. 5

    d. 15

    e. 16

19. Six people apply to work for Janice's company, but she only needs four workers. How many different groups of four employees can Janice choose?

    a. 6

    b. 10

    c. 15

    d. 36

    e. 30

20. If $f(x) = (\frac{1}{2})^x$ and $a < b$, then which of the following must be true?

    a. $f(a) < f(b)$
    b. $f(a) > f(b)$
    c. $f(a) + f(b) = 0$
    d $3f(a) = f(b)$
    e. $f(a) = f(b) + 1$

Answer Explanations

1. B: The determinant of a 2 x 2 matrix is $ad - bc$. The calculation is -4(-1) − 2(3) = 4 − 6 = -2.

2. B: $\frac{2}{a}$ must be subtracted from both sides, with a result of $\frac{1}{x} = \frac{2}{b} - \frac{2}{a}$. The reciprocal of both sides needs to be taken, but the right-hand side needs to be written as a single fraction in order to do that. Since the two fractions on the right have denominators that are not equal, a common denominator of ab is needed. This leaves $\frac{1}{x} = \frac{2a}{ab} - \frac{2b}{ab} = \frac{2(a-b)}{ab}$. Taking the reciprocals, which can be done since $b - a$ is not zero, with a result of $x = \frac{ab}{2(a-b)}$.

3. B: Plugging into the quadratic formula yields, for solutions $x = \frac{1 \pm \sqrt{-1 + 4 \cdot 1(-3)}}{2} = \frac{1}{2} \pm \frac{\sqrt{11}}{2}$. Therefore, $x - \frac{1}{2} = \pm \frac{\sqrt{11}}{2}$. Now, if this is squared, then the $\pm$ cancels and left with $\left(\frac{\sqrt{11}}{2}\right)^2 = \frac{11}{4}$.

4. A: Parallel lines have the same slope. The slope of C can be seen to be 1/3 by dividing both sides by 3. For E, divide both sides by 2 and see the slope is 3/2. The others are in standard form $Ax + By = C$, for which the slope is given by $\frac{-A}{B}$. The slope of A is 3, the slope of B is 4. The slope of D is 1.

5. B: The slope will be given by $\frac{1-0}{2-0} = \frac{1}{2}$. The y-intercept will be 0, since it passes through the origin. Using slope-intercept form, the equation for this line is $y = \frac{1}{2}x$.

6. C: Let r be the number of red cans and b be the number of blue cans. One equation is $r + b = 10$. The total price is $16, and the prices for each can means $1r + 2b = 16$. Multiplying the first equation on both sides by -1 results in $-r - b = -10$. Add this equation to the second equation, leaving $b = 6$. So, she bought 6 *blue* cans. From the first equation, this means r = 4; thus, she bought 4 *red* cans.

7. E: The first field has an area of 1000 feet, so the length of one side is $\sqrt{1000} = 10\sqrt{10}$. Since there are four sides to a square, the total perimeter is $40\sqrt{10}$. The second square has an area of 10 square feet, so the length of one side is $\sqrt{10}$, and the total perimeter is $4\sqrt{10}$. Adding these together gives $40\sqrt{10} + 4\sqrt{10} = (40 + 4)\sqrt{10} = 44\sqrt{10}$.

8. C: If $\log_{10} x = 2$, then $10^2 = x$, which equals 100.

9. B: Recall that to compose functions, replace the x in the expression for g with the expression for f everywhere there is x. So $g(f(x)) = \frac{f(x)-1}{4} = \frac{2x+1-1}{4} = \frac{2x}{4} = \frac{x}{2}$.

10. A: For acute angles, the only angle for which $\sin\theta = \frac{\sqrt{3}}{2}$ is $\frac{\pi}{3}$. Also, $\cos\frac{\pi}{3} = \frac{1}{2}$.

11. C: The $(3x + 1)$ can be factored to get $(2x - 5)(3x + 1)$.

12. E: Because the coefficient of x^2 is negative, this function has a graph that is a parabola that opens downward. Therefore, it will be greater than 0 between its real roots, if it has any. Checking the discriminant, the result is $1^2 - 4(-3)(-8) = 1 - 96 = -95$. Since the discriminant is negative, this equation has no real solutions. Since this has no real roots, it must be always positive or always negative. Its graph opens downward, so it has at least some negative values. That means it is always negative. Thus, it is bigger than zero for no real numbers.

13. A: Check each value, but it is easiest to use the quadratic formula, which gives $x = \frac{2 \pm \sqrt{(-2)^2 - 4(1)(-2)}}{2} = 1 \pm \frac{\sqrt{12}}{2} = 1 \pm \frac{2\sqrt{3}}{2} = 1 \pm \sqrt{3}$. The only one of these which appears as an answer choice is $1 + \sqrt{3}$.

14. B: The y coordinate of every point on the graph of $y = x^2 + 2$ has a vertex at (0,2) on the y-axis. The circle with a center at (0,1) also lies on the y-axis. With a radius of 1, the circle touches the parabola at one point. The vertex of the parabola (0,2).

15. D: The slope is given by the change in y divided by the change in x. The change in y is 2-0 = 2, and the change in x is $0 - (-4) = 4$. The slope is $\frac{2}{4} = \frac{1}{2}$.

16. B: The number of ways to order n objects is given by the product $\binom{n}{1}\binom{n-1}{1} \ldots \binom{1}{1}$. This is $\binom{3}{1}\binom{2}{1}\binom{1}{1} = \frac{3!}{1!2!} \cdot \frac{2!}{1!1!} \cdot \frac{1!}{1!1!}$. 1! is just 1, and the 2! in the numerator and denominator will cancel one another, with a result of $3! = 3 \cdot 2 \cdot 1 = 6$.

17. C: If $y = f^{-1}(6)$ then y must satisfy $f(y) = 6$. Substituting and solving for y yields $4y + 2 = 6$, then $4y = 4$, and $y = 1$.

18. C: Find $a_2 = 3a_1 - 1 = 3 \cdot 1 - 1 = 2$. Next, find $a_3 = 3a_2 - 1 = 3 \cdot 2 - 1 = 5$.

19. C: Janice will be choosing 4 employees out of a set of 6 applicants, so this will be given by the choice function. The following equation shows the choice function worked out: $\binom{6}{4} = \frac{6!}{4!(6-4)!} = \frac{6!}{4!(2)!} = \frac{6 \cdot 5 \cdot 4 \cdot 3 \cdot 2 \cdot 1}{4 \cdot 3 \cdot 2 \cdot 1 \cdot 2 \cdot 1} = \frac{6 \cdot 5}{2} = 15$.

20. B: Here, f is an exponential function whose base is less than 1. In this function, f is always decreasing. This means that when a is less than b, $f(a) > f(b)$.

Elementary Algebra

Computation with Integers and Negative Rational Numbers

Integers are the whole numbers together with their negatives. They include numbers like 5, 24, 0, -6, and 15. They do not include fractions or numbers that have digits after the decimal point.

Rational numbers are all numbers that can be written as a fraction using integers. A *fraction* is written as $\frac{x}{y}$ and represents the quotient of *x* being divided by *y*. More practically, it means dividing the whole into *y* equal parts, then taking *x* of those parts.

Examples of rational numbers include $\frac{1}{2}$ and $\frac{5}{4}$. The number on the top is called the *numerator*, and the number on the bottom is called the *denominator*. Because every integer can be written as a fraction with a denominator of 1, (e.g. $\frac{3}{1} = 3$), every integer is also a rational number.

When adding integers and negative rational numbers, there are some basic rules to determine if the solution is negative or positive:

Adding two positive numbers results in a positive number: 3.3 + 4.8 = 8.1.

Adding two negative numbers results in a negative number: (-8) + (-6) = -14.

Adding one positive and one negative number requires taking the absolute values and finding the difference between them. Then, the sign of the number that has the higher absolute value for the final solution is used.

For example, (-9) + 11, has a difference of absolute values of 2. The final solution is 2 because 11 has the higher absolute value. Another example is 9 + (-11), which has a difference of absolute values of 2. The final solution is -2 because 11 has the higher absolute value.

When subtracting integers and negative rational numbers, one has to change the problem to adding the opposite and then apply the rules of addition.

Subtracting two positive numbers is the same as adding one positive and one negative number.

For example, 4.9 – 7.1 is the same as 4.9 + (-7.1). The solution is -2.2 since the absolute value of -7.1 is greater. Another example is 8.5 – 6.4 which is the same as 8.5 + (-6.4). The solution is 2.1 since the absolute value of 8.5 is greater.

Subtracting a positive number from a negative number results in negative value.

For example, (-12) – 7 is the same as (-12) + (-7) with a solution of -19.

Subtracting a negative number from a positive number results in a positive value.

For example, 12 – (-7) is the same as 12 + 7 with a solution of 19.

For multiplication and division of integers and rational numbers, if both numbers are positive or both numbers are negative, the result is a positive value.

For example, (-1.7)(-4) has a solution of 6.8 since both numbers are negative values.

If one number is positive and another number is negative, the result is a negative value.

For example, (-15)/5 has a solution of -3 since there is one negative number.

The Use of Absolute Values

The *absolute value* represents the distance a number is from 0. The *absolute value symbol* is | | with a number between the bars. The |10| = 10 and the |-10| = 10.

When simplifying an algebraic expression, the value of the absolute value expression is determined first, much like parenthesis in the order of operations. See the example below:

$$|8 - 12| + 5 = |\text{-}4| + 5 = 4 + 5 = 9$$

Ordering

Exponents are shorthand for longer multiplications or divisions. The exponent is written to the upper right of a number. In the expression 2^3, the exponent is 3. The number with the exponent is called the *base*.

When the exponent is a whole number, it means to multiply the base by itself as many times as the number in the exponent. So, $2^3 = 2 \times 2 \times 2 = 8$.

If the exponent is a negative number, it means to take the reciprocal of the positive exponent:

$$2^{-3} = \frac{1}{2^3} = \frac{1}{8}$$

When the exponent is 0, the result is always 1: $2^0 = 1, 5^0 = 1$, and so on.

When the exponent is 2, the number is *squared*, and when the exponent is 3, it is *cubed*.

When working with longer expressions, parentheses are used to show the order in which the operations should be performed. Operations inside the parentheses should be completed first. Thus, $(3 - 1) \div 2$ means one should first subtract 1 from 3, and then divide that result by 2.

The *order of operations* gives an order for how a mathematical expression is to be simplified:

- Parentheses
- Exponents
- Multiplication
- Division
- Addition
- Subtraction

To help remember this, many students like to use the mnemonic PEMDAS. Some students associate this word with a phrase to help them, such as "Pirates Eat Many Donuts at Sea." Here is a quick example:

$$\text{Evaluate } 2^2 \times (3 - 1) \div 2 + 3.$$

$$\text{Parenthesis: } 2^2 \times 2 \div 2 + 3.$$

$$\text{Exponents: } 4 \times 2 \div 2 + 3$$

$$\text{Multiply: } 8 \div 2 + 3.$$

$$\text{Divide: } 4 + 3.$$

$$\text{Addition: } 7$$

Evaluation of Simple Formulas and Expressions

To evaluate simple formulas and expressions, the first step is to substitute the given values in for the variable(s). Then, the order of operations is used to simplify.

Example 1
Evaluate $\frac{1}{2}x^2 - 3, x = 4$.

The first step is to substitute in 4 for x in the expression: $\frac{1}{2}(4)^2 - 3$.

Then, the order of operations is used to simplify.

The exponent comes first, $\frac{1}{2}(16) - 3$, then the multiplication $8 - 3$, and then, after subtraction, the solution is 5.

Example 2
Evaluate $4|5 - x| + 2y, x = 4, y = -3$.

The first step is to substitute 4 in for x and -3 in for y in the expression: $4|5 - 4| + 2(-3)$.

Then, the absolute value expression is simplified, which is $|5 - 4| = |1| = 1$.

The expression is $4(1) + 2(-3)$ which can be simplified using the order of operations.

First is the multiplication, 4 + (-6); then addition yields an answer of -2.

Example 3
Find the perimeter of a rectangle with a length of 6 inches and a width of 9 inches.

The first step is substituting in 6 for the length and 9 for the width in the perimeter of a rectangle formula, $P = 2(6) + 2(9)$.

Then, the order of operations is used to simplify.

First is multiplication (resulting in 12 + 21) and then addition for a solution of 33 inches.

Adding and Subtracting Monomials and Polynomials

To add or subtract polynomials, add the coefficients of terms with the same exponent. For instance, $(-2x^2 + 3x + 1) + (4x^2 - x) = (-2 + 4)x^2 + (3 - 1)x + 1 = 2x^2 + 2x + 1$.

Multiplying and Dividing Monomials and Polynomials

To multiply polynomials each term of the first polynomial multiplies each term of the second polynomial, and adds up the results. Here's an example:

$$(3x^4 + 2x^2)(2x^2 + 3) = 3x^4 \cdot 2x^2 + 3x^4 \cdot 3 + 2x^2 \cdot 2x^2 + 2x^2 \cdot 3$$

Then, add like terms with a result of:

$$6x^6 + 9x^4 + 4x^4 + 6x^2 = 6x^6 + 13x^4 + 6x^2$$

A polynomial with two terms is called a *binomial*. Another way of remember the rule for multiplying two binomials is to use the acronym *FOIL*: multiply the *First* terms together, then the *Outside* terms (terms on the far left and far right), then the *Inner* terms, and finally the *Last* two terms. For longer polynomials, there is no such convenient mnemonic, so remember to multiply each term of the first polynomial by each term of the second, and add the results.

To divide one polynomial by another, the procedure is similar to long division. At each step, one needs to figure out how to get the term of the dividend with the highest exponent as a multiple of the divisor. The divisor is multiplied by the multiple to get that term, which goes in the quotient. Then, the product of this term is subtracted with the dividend from the divisor and repeat the process. This sounds rather abstract, so it may be easiest to see the procedure by describing it while looking at an example.

Example
$(4x^3 + x^2 - x + 4) \div (2x - 1)$

The first step is to cancel out the highest term in the first polynomial.

To get $4x^3$ from the second polynomial, multiply by $2x^2$.

The first term for the quotient is going to be $2x^2$.

The result of $2x^2(2x - 1)$ is $4x^3 - 2x^2$. Subtract this from the first polynomial.

The result is $(-x^2 - x + 4) \div (2x - 1)$.

The procedure is repeated: to cancel the $-x^2$ term, then multiply $(2x - 1)$ by $-\frac{1}{2}x$.

Adding this to the quotient, the quotient becomes $2x^2 - \frac{1}{2}x$.

The dividend is changed by subtracting $-\frac{1}{2}x(2x - 1)$ from it to obtain $(-\frac{3}{2}x + 4) \div (2x - 1)$.

To get $-\frac{3}{2}x$ needs to be multiplied by $-\frac{3}{4}$.

The quotient, therefore, becomes $2x^2 - \frac{1}{2}x - \frac{3}{4}$.

The remaining part is $4.75 \div (2x - 1)$.

There is no monomial to multiply to cancel this constant term, since the divisor now has a higher power than the dividend.

The final answer is the quotient plus the remainder divided by $(2x - 1)$: $2x^2 - \frac{1}{2}x - \frac{3}{4} + \frac{4.75}{2x-1}$.

The Evaluation of Positive Rational Roots and Exponents

There are a few rules for working with exponents. For any numbers $a, b, m, n,$ the following hold true:

$$a^1 = a$$

$$1^a = 1$$

$$a^0 = 1$$

$$a^m \times a^n = a^{m+n}$$

$$a^m \div a^n = a^{m-n}$$

$$(a^m)^n = a^{m \times n}$$

$$(a \times b)^m = a^m \times b^m$$

$$(a \div b)^m = a^m \div b^m$$

Any number, including a fraction, can be an exponent. The same rules apply.

Simplifying Algebraic Fractions

A *rational expression* is a fraction with a polynomial in the numerator and denominator. The denominator polynomial cannot be zero. An example of a rational expression is $\frac{3x^4 - 2}{-x + 1}$. The same rules for working with addition, subtraction, multiplication, and division with rational expressions apply as when working with regular fractions.

The first step is to find a common denominator when adding or subtracting. This can be done just as with regular fractions. For example, if $\frac{a}{b} + \frac{c}{d}$, then a common denominator can be found by multiplying to find the following fractions: $\frac{ad}{bd}, \frac{cb}{db}$.

A *complex fraction* is a fraction in which the numerator and denominator are themselves fractions, of the form $\frac{\left(\frac{a}{b}\right)}{\left(\frac{c}{d}\right)}$. These can be simplified by following the usual rules for the order of operations, or by remembering that dividing one fraction by another is the same as multiplying by the reciprocal of the divisor. This means that any complex fraction can be rewritten using the following form: $\frac{\left(\frac{a}{b}\right)}{\left(\frac{c}{d}\right)} = \frac{a}{b} \cdot \frac{d}{c}$.

The following problem is an example of solving a complex fraction:

$$\frac{\left(\frac{5}{4}\right)}{\left(\frac{3}{8}\right)} = \frac{5}{4} \cdot \frac{8}{3} = \frac{40}{12} = \frac{10}{3}$$

Factoring

Factors for polynomials are similar to factors for integers. One polynomial is a factor of a second polynomial if the second polynomial can be obtained from the first by multiplying by a third polynomial. $6x^6 + 13x^4 + 6x^2$ can be obtained by multiplying $(3x^4 + 2x^2)$ and $(2x^2 + 3)$ together. This means $2x^2 + 3$ and $3x^4 + 2x^2$ are factors of $6x^6 + 13x^4 + 6x^2$.

In general, finding the factors of a polynomial can be tricky. However, there are a few types of polynomials that can be factored in a straightforward way. If a certain monomial divides each term of a polynomial, it can be factored out:

$$x^2 + 2xy + y^2 = (x + y)^2$$

$$x^2 - 2xy + y^2 = (x - y)^2$$

$$x^2 - y^2 = (x + y)(x - y)$$

$$x^3 + y^3 = (x + y)(x^2 - xy + y^2)$$

$$x^3 - y^3 = (x - y)(x^2 + xy + y^2)$$

$$x^3 + 3x^2y + 3xy^2 + y^3 = (x + y)^3$$

$$x^3 - 3x^2y + 3xy^2 - y^3 = (x - y)^3$$

These rules can be used in many combinations with one another. To give one example, the expression $3x^3 - 24$ factors to

$$3(x^3 - 8) = 3(x - 2)(x^2 + 2x + 4)$$

When factoring polynomials, it is a good idea to multiply the factors to check the result.

Solving Linear Equations and Inequalities

The simplest equations to solve are *linear equations*, which have the form $ax + b = 0$. These have the solution $x = -\frac{b}{a}$.

For instance, in the equation $\frac{1}{3}x - 4 = 0$, it can be determined that $\frac{1}{3}x = 4$ by adding 4 on each side. Next, both sides of the equation are multiplied by 3 to get $x = 12$.

Solving an inequality is very similar to solving equations, with one important issue to keep track of: if multiplying or dividing both sides of an inequality by a negative number, the direction of the inequality *flips*.

For example, consider the inequality $-4x < 12$. Solving this inequality requires the division of -4. When the negative four is divided, the less-than sign changes to a greater-than sign. The solution becomes $x > -3$.

Example
$-4x - 3 \leq -2x + 1$

2x is added to both sides, and 3 is added to both sides, leaving $-2x \leq 4$.

$-2x \leq 4$ is multiplied by $-\frac{1}{2}$, which means flipping the direction of the inequality.

This gives $x \geq -2$.

An *absolute inequality* is an inequality that is true for all real numbers. An inequality that is only true for some real numbers is called *conditional*.

In addition to the inequalities above, there are also *double inequalities* where three quantities are compared to one another, such as $3 \leq x + 4 < 5$. The rules for double inequalities include always performing any operations to every part of the inequality and reversing the direction of the inequality when multiplying or dividing by a negative number.

When solving equations and inequalities, the solutions can be checked by plugging the answer back in to the original problem. If the solution makes a true statement, the solution is correct.

Solving Quadratic Equations by Factoring

Solving quadratic equations is a little trickier. If they take the form $ax^2 - b = 0$, then the equation can be solved by adding b to both sides and dividing by a to get $x^2 = \frac{b}{a}$.

Using the sixth rule above, the solution is $x = \pm\sqrt{\frac{b}{a}}$. Note that this is actually two separate solutions, unless b happens to be 0.

If a quadratic equation has no constant—so that it takes the form $ax^2 + bx = 0$—then the x can be factored out to get $x(ax + b) = 0$. Then, the solutions are $x = 0$, together with the solutions to $ax + b = 0$. Both factors x and $(ax + b)$ can be set equal to zero to solve for x because one of those values must be zero for their product to equal zero. For an equation $ab = 0$ to be true, either $a = 0$, or $b = 0$.

A given quadratic equation $x^2 + bx + c$ can be factored into $(x + A)(x + B)$, where $A + B = b$, and $AB = c$. Finding the values of A and B can take time, but such a pair of numbers can be found by guessing and checking. Looking at the positive and negative factors for c offers a good starting point.

For example, in $x^2 - 5x + 6$, the factors of 6 are 1, 2, and 3. Now, $(-2)(-3) = 6$, and $-2 - 3 = -5$. In general, however, this may not work, in which case another approach may need to be used.

A quadratic equation of the form $x^2 + 2xb + b^2 = 0$ can be factored into $(x + b)^2 = 0$. Similarly, $x^2 - 2xy + y^2 = 0$ factors into $(x - y)^2 = 0$.

In general, the constant term may not be the right value to be factored this way. A more general method for solving these quadratic equations must then be found. The following two methods will work in any situation.

Completing the Square

The first method is called *completing the square*. The idea here is that in any equation $x^2 + 2xb + c = 0$, something could be added to both sides of the equation to get the left side to look like $x^2 + 2xb + b^2$, meaning it could be factored into $(x + b)^2 = 0$.

Example
$x^2 + 6x - 1 = 0$

The left-hand side could be factored if the constant were equal to 9, , since $x^2 + 6x + 9 = (x + 3)^2$.

To get a constant of 9 on the left, 10 needs to be added to both sides.

That changes the equation to $x^2 + 6x + 9 = 10$.

Factoring the left gives $(x + 3)^2 = 10$.

Then, the square root of both sides can be taken (remembering that this introduces a $\pm$): $x + 3 = \pm\sqrt{10}$.

Finally, 3 is subtracted from both sides to get two solutions: $x = -3 \pm \sqrt{10}$.

The Quadratic Formula

The first method of completing the square can be used in finding the second method, the quadratic formula. It can be used to solve any quadratic equation. This formula may be the longest method for solving quadratic equations and is commonly used as a last resort after other methods are ruled out.

It can be helpful in memorizing the formula to see where it comes from, so here are the steps involved.

The most general form for a quadratic equation is $ax^2 + bx + c = 0$.

First, dividing both sides by a leaves with $x^2 + \frac{b}{a}x + \frac{c}{a} = 0$.

To complete the square on the left hand side, c/a can be subtracted on both sides to get $x^2 + \frac{b}{a}x = -\frac{c}{a}$.

$(\frac{b}{2a})^2$ is then added to both sides.

This gives $x^2 + \frac{b}{a}x + (\frac{b}{2a})^2 = (\frac{b}{2a})^2 - \frac{c}{a}$.

The left can now be factored and the right hand side simplified to give $(x + \frac{b}{2a})^2 = \frac{b^2 - 4ac}{4a}$.

Taking the square roots gives $x + \frac{b}{2a} = \pm\frac{\sqrt{b^2 - 4ac}}{2a}$.

Solving for x yields the quadratic formula: $x = \frac{-b \pm \sqrt{b^2 - 4ac}}{2a}$.

It isn't necessary to remember how to get this formula, but memorizing the formula itself is the goal.

If an equation involves taking a root, then the first step is to move the root to one side of the equation and everything else to the other side. That way, both sides can be raised to the index of the radical in order to remove it, and solving the equation can continue.

Solving Verbal Problems Presented in an Algebraic Context

There is a four-step process in problem-solving that can be used as a guide:

1. Understand the problem and determine the unknown information.

2. Translate the verbal problem into an algebraic equation.

3. Solve the equation by using inverse operations.

4. Check the work and answer the given question.

Example
Three times the sum of a number plus 4 equals the number plus 8. What is the number?

The first step is to determine the unknown, which is the number, or x.

The second step is to translate the problem into the equation, which is $3(x + 4) = x + 8$.

The equation can be solved as follows:

$3x + 12 = x + 8$	Apply the distributive property
$3x = x - 4$	Subtract 12 from both sides of the equation
$2x = -4$	Subtract x from both sides of the equation
$x = -2$	Divide both sides of the equation by 2

The final step is checking the solution. Plugging the value for x back into the equation yields the following problem: $3(-2) + 12 = -2 + 8$. Using the order of operations shows that a true statement is made: $6 = 6$

Geometric Reasoning and Graphing

The four-step process of problem solving can be used with geometric reasoning problems as well. There are many geometric properties and terminology included within geometric reasoning.

For example, the perimeter of a rectangle can be written in the terms of the width, or the width can be written in terms of the length.

Example
The width of a rectangle is 2 centimeters less than the length. If the perimeter of the rectangle is 44 centimeters, then what are the dimensions of a rectangle?

The first step is to determine the unknown, which is in terms of the length, l.

The second step is to translate the problem into the equation using the perimeter of a rectangle, $P = 2l + 2w$. The width is the length minus 2 centimeters. The resulting equation is $2l + 2(l - 2) = 44$. The equation can be solved as follows:

$2l + 2l - 4 = 44$	Apply the distributive property on the left side of the equation
$4l - 4 = 44$	Combine like terms on the left side of the equation
$4l = 48$	Add 4 to both sides of the equation
$l = 12$	Divide both sides of the equation by 4

The length of the rectangle is 12 centimeters. The width is the length minus 2 centimeters, which is 10 centimeters. Checking the answers for length and width forms the following equation: $44 = 2(12) + 2(10)$. The equation can be solved using the order of operations to form a true statement: $44 = 44$.

Equations can also be created from complementary angles (angles that add up to 90°) and supplementary angles (angles that add up to 180°).

Example
Two angles are complementary. If one angle is four times the other angle, what is the measure of each angle?

The first step is to determine the unknown, which is the measure of the angle.

The second step is to translate the problem into the equation using the known statement: the sum of two complementary angles is 90°. The resulting equation is $4x + x = 90$. The equation can be solved as follows:

$5x = 90$	Combine like terms on the left side of the equation
$x = 18$	Divide both sides of the equation by 5

The first angle is 18° and the second angle is 4 times the unknown, which is 4 times 18 or 72°.

Going back to check the answer with the original question, 72 and 18 have a sum of 90, making them complimentary angles. Seventy-two degrees is also four times the other angle, 18 degrees.

Translation of Written Phases into Algebraic Expressions

An *algebraic expression* contains one or more operations and one or more variables. To convert written phrases into algebraic expression, there are some key terms to recognize:

- Key terms with addition are *sum, increase, plus, add, more than*, and *total*.
- Key terms with subtraction are *difference, decrease, minus, subtract*, and *less than*.
- Key terms with multiplication are *product, times*, and *multiplied*.
- Key terms with division are *quotient, divided*, and *ratio*.
- Key terms with exponent are *squares, cubed*, and *raised to a power*.

To write a phrase as an algebraic expression, it's necessary to identify the unknown(s) where variables will be used and the words for the correct operation.

<u>Example 1</u>
Write an expression for three times the sum of twice the number *n* plus five.

Three times means *3 x*, twice a number and five means *2n + 5*, and the final expression is *3(2n + 5)*.

<u>Example 2</u>
Write an expression for the total price of $2 per pound for grapes and $3 per pound for strawberries.

The total means the sum. The price for grapes is *2g*, and the price for strawberries is *3s*. The expression is *2g + 3s*.

Practice Questions

1. What is the value of $x^2 - 2xy + 2y^2$ when $x = 2, y = 3$?
   a. 8
   b. 10
   c. 12
   d. 14

2. $(2x - 4y)^2 =$
   a. $4x^2 - 16xy + 16y^2$
   b. $4x^2 - 8xy + 16y^2$
   c. $4x^2 - 16xy - 16y^2$
   d. $2x^2 - 8xy + 8y^2$

3. If $x > 3$, then $\frac{x^2 - 6x + 9}{x^2 - x - 6} =$
   a. $\frac{x+2}{x-3}$
   b. $\frac{x-2}{x-3}$
   c. $\frac{x-3}{x+3}$
   d. $\frac{x-3}{x+2}$

4. The square and circle have the same center. The circle has a radius of r. What is the area of the shaded region?

   a. $r^2 - \pi r^2$
   b. $4r^2 - 2\pi r$
   c. $(4 - \pi)r^2$
   d. $(\pi - 1)r^2$

5. If $4x - 3 = 5$, then $x =$
   a. 1
   b. 2
   c. 3
   d. 4

6. Solve for x, if $x^2 - 2x - 8 = 0$.

   a. $2 \pm \frac{\sqrt{30}}{2}$

   b. $2 \pm 4\sqrt{2}$

   c. 1 ± 3

   d. $4 \pm \sqrt{2}$

7. Which of the following is a factor of both $x^2 + 4x + 4$ and $x^2 - x - 6$?

   a. $x - 3$

   b. $x + 2$

   c. $x - 2$

   d. $x + 3$

8. Write the expression for three times the sum of twice a number and one minus 6.

   a. $2x + 1 - 6$

   b. $3x + 1 - 6$

   c. $3(x + 1) - 6$

   d. $3(2x + 1) - 6$

9. On Monday, Robert mopped the floor in 4 hours. On Tuesday, he did it in 3 hours. If on Monday, his average rate of mopping was p sq. ft. per hour, what was his average rate on Tuesday?

   a. $\frac{4}{3}p$ sq. ft. per hour

   b. $\frac{3}{4}p$ sq. ft. per hour

   c. $\frac{5}{4}p$ sq. ft. per hour

   d. $p + 1$ sq. ft. per hour

10. Which of the following inequalities is equivalent to $3 - \frac{1}{2}x \geq 2$?

   a. $x \geq 2$

   b. $x \leq 2$

   c. $x \geq 1$

   d. $x \leq 1$

11. For which of the following are $x = 4$ and $x = -4$ solutions?

   a. $x^2 + 16 = 0$

   b. $x^2 + 4x - 4 = 0$

   c. $x^2 - 2x - 2 = 0$

   d. $x^2 - 16 = 0$

12. If x is not zero, then $\frac{3}{x} + \frac{5u}{2x} - \frac{u}{4} =$

a. $\frac{12+10u-ux}{4x}$

b. $\frac{3+5u-ux}{x}$

c. $\frac{12x+10u+ux}{4x}$

d. $\frac{12+10u-u}{4x}$

Answer Explanations

1. B: Each instance of x is replaced with a 2, and each instance of y is replaced with a 3 to get $2^2 - 2 \cdot 2 \cdot 3 + 2 \cdot 3^2 = 4 - 12 + 18 = 10$.

2. A: To expand a squared binomial, it's necessary use the *First, Inner, Outer, Last Method*. $(2x - 4y)^2 = 2x \cdot 2x + 2x(-4y) + (-4y)(2x) + (-4y)(-4y) = 4x^2 - 8xy - 8xy + 16y^2 = 4x^2 - 16xy + 16y^2$.

3. D: Factor the numerator into $x^2 - 6x + 9 = (x - 3)^2$, since $-3 - 3 = -6, (-3)(-3) = 9$. Factor the denominator into $x^2 - x - 6 = (x - 3)(x + 2)$, since $-3 + 2 = -1, (-3)(2) = -6$. This means the rational function can be rewritten as $\frac{x^2-6x+9}{x^2-x-6} = \frac{(x-3)^2}{(x-3)(x+2)}$. Using the restriction of x > 3, do not worry about any of these terms being 0, and cancel an $x - 3$ from the numerator and the denominator, leaving $\frac{x-3}{x+2}$.

4. C: The area of the shaded region is the area of the square, minus the area of the circle. The area of the circle will be πr^2. The side of the square will be $2r$, so the area of the square will be $4r^2$. Therefore, the difference is $4r^2 - \pi r^2 = (4 - \pi)r^2$.

5. B: Add 3 to both sides to get $4x = 8$. Then divide both sides by 4 to get $x = 2$.

6. C: The numbers needed are those that add to -2 and multiply to -8. The difference between 2 and 4 is 2. Their product is 8, and -4 and 2 will work. Therefore, $x^2 - 2x - 8 = (x - 4)(x + 2)$. The latter has roots 4 and -2 or 1 ± 3.

7. B: To factor $x^2 + 4x + 4$, the numbers needed are those that add to 4 and multiply to 4. Therefore, both numbers must be 2, and the expression factors to $x^2 + 4x + 4 = (x + 2)^2$. Similarly, the expression factors to $x^2 - x - 6 = (x - 3)(x + 2)$, so that they have $x + 2$ in common.

8. D: The expression is three times the sum of twice a number and 1, which is $3(2x + 1)$. Then, 6 is subtracted from this expression.

9. A: Robert accomplished his task on Tuesday in ¾ the time compared to Monday. He must have worked 4/3 as fast.

10. B: To simplify this inequality, subtract 3 from both sides to get $-\frac{1}{2}x \geq -1$. Then, multiply both sides by -2 (remembering this flips the direction of the inequality) to get $x \leq 2$.

11. D: There are two ways to approach this problem. Each value can be substituted into each equation. A can be eliminated, since $4^2 + 16 = 32$. Choice *B* can be eliminated, since $4^2 + 4 \cdot 4 - 4 = 28$. *C* can be eliminated, since $4^2 - 2 \cdot 4 - 2 = 6$. But, plugging in either value into $x^2 - 16$, which gives $(\pm 4)^2 - 16 = 16 - 16 = 0$.

12. C: The common denominator here will be 4x. Rewrite these fractions as $\frac{3}{x} + \frac{5u}{2x} - \frac{u}{4} = \frac{12}{4x} + \frac{10u}{4x} - \frac{ux}{4x} = \frac{12x+10u+ux}{4x}$.

Reading Comprehension Test

The Purpose of a Passage

No matter the genre or format, all authors are writing to persuade, inform, entertain, or express feelings. Often, these purposes are blended, with one dominating the rest. It's useful to learn to recognize the author's intent.

Persuasive writing is used to persuade or convince readers of something. It often contains two elements: the argument and the counterargument. The argument takes a stance on an issue, while the counterargument pokes holes in the opposition's stance. Authors rely on logic, emotion, and writer credibility to persuade readers to agree with them. If readers are opposed to the stance before reading, they are unlikely to adopt that stance. However, those who are undecided or committed to the same stance are more likely to agree with the author.

Informative writing tries to teach or inform. Workplace manuals, instructor lessons, statistical reports and cookbooks are examples of informative texts. Informative writing is usually based on facts and is often void of emotion and persuasion. Informative texts generally contain statistics, charts, and graphs. Though most informative texts lack a persuasive agenda, readers must examine the text carefully to determine whether one exists within a given passage.

Stories or narratives are designed to entertain. When you go to the movies, you often want to escape for a few hours, not necessarily to think critically. Entertaining writing is designed to delight and engage the reader. However, sometimes this type of writing can be woven into more serious materials, such as persuasive or informative writing to hook the reader before transitioning into a more scholarly discussion.

Emotional writing works to evoke the reader's feelings, such as anger, euphoria, or sadness. The connection between reader and author is an attempt to cause the reader to share the author's intended emotion or tone. Sometimes in order to make a piece more poignant, the author simply wants readers to feel emotion that the author has felt. Other times, the author attempts to persuade or manipulate the reader into adopting his stance. While it's okay to sympathize with the author, be aware of the individual's underlying intent.

Types of Passages

Writing can be classified under four passage types: narrative, expository, technical, and persuasive. Though these types are not mutually exclusive, one form tends to dominate the rest. By recognizing the *type* of passage you're reading, you gain insight into *how* you should read. If you're reading a narrative, you can assume the author intends to entertain, which means you may skim the text without losing meaning. A technical document might require a close read, because skimming the passage might cause the reader to miss salient details.

1. *Narrative* writing, at its core, is the art of storytelling. For a narrative to exist, certain elements must be present. It must have characters. While many characters are human, characters could be defined as anything that thinks, acts, and talks like a human. For example, many recent movies, such as *Lord of the Rings* and *The Chronicles of Narnia*, include animals, fantastical creatures, and even trees that behave like humans. It must have a plot or sequence of events. Typically, those events follow a standard plot diagram, but recent trends start *in medias res* or in the middle (near the climax). In this instance,

foreshadowing and flashbacks often fill in plot details. Along with characters and a plot, there must also be conflict. Conflict is usually divided into two types: internal and external. Internal conflict indicates the character is in turmoil. Internal conflicts are presented through the character's thoughts. External conflicts are visible. Types of external conflict include a person versus nature, another person, and society.

2. *Expository* writing is detached and to the point, while other types of writing—persuasive, narrative, and descriptive—are lively. Since expository writing is designed to instruct or inform, it usually involves directions and steps written in second person ("you" voice) and lacks any persuasive or narrative elements. Sequence words such as *first*, *second*, and *third*, or *in the first place*, *secondly*, and *lastly* are often given to add fluency and cohesion. Common examples of expository writing include instructor's lessons, cookbook recipes, and repair manuals.

3. Due to its empirical nature, *technical* writing is filled with steps, charts, graphs, data, and statistics. The goal of technical writing is to advance understanding in a field through the scientific method. Experts such as teachers, doctors, or mechanics use words unique to the profession in which they operate. These words, which often incorporate acronyms, are called *jargon*. Technical writing is a type of expository writing, but is not meant to be understood by the general public. Instead, technical writers assume readers have received a formal education in a particular field of study, and need no explanation as to what the jargon means. Imagine a doctor trying to understand a diagnostic reading for a car or a mechanic trying to interpret lab results. Only professionals with proper training will fully comprehend the text.

4. *Persuasive* writing is designed to change opinions and attitudes. The topic, stance, and arguments are found in the thesis, positioned near the end of the introduction. Later supporting paragraphs offer relevant quotations, paraphrases, and summaries from primary or secondary sources, which are then interpreted, analyzed, and evaluated. The goal of persuasive writers is not to stack quotes, but to develop original ideas by using sources as a starting point. Good persuasive writing makes powerful arguments with valid sources and thoughtful analysis. Poor persuasive writing is riddled with bias and logical fallacies. Sometimes, logical and illogical arguments are sandwiched together in the same piece. Therefore, readers should display skepticism when reading persuasive arguments.

Text Structure

Depending on what the author is attempting to accomplish, certain formats or text structures work better than others. For example, a sequence structure might work for narration but not when identifying similarities and differences between dissimilar concepts. Similarly, a comparison-contrast structure is not useful for narration. It's the author's job to put the right information in the correct format.

Readers should be familiar with the five main literary structures:

1. *Sequence* structure (sometimes referred to as the order structure) is when the order of events proceed in a predictable order. In many cases, this means the text goes through the plot elements: exposition, rising action, climax, falling action, and resolution. Readers are introduced to characters, setting, and conflict in the exposition. In the rising action, there's an increase in tension and suspense. The climax is the height of tension and the point of no return. Tension decreases during the falling action. In the resolution, any conflicts presented in the exposition are solved, and the story concludes. An informative text that is structured sequentially will often go in order from one step to the next.

2. In the *problem-solution* structure, authors identify a potential problem and suggest a solution. This form of writing is usually divided into two paragraphs and can be found in informational texts. For example, cell phone, cable and satellite providers use this structure in manuals to help customers troubleshoot or identify problems with services or products.

3. When authors want to discuss similarities and differences between separate concepts, they arrange thoughts in a *comparison-contrast* paragraph structure. Venn diagrams are an effective graphic organizer for comparison-contrast structures, because they feature two overlapping circles that can be used to organize similarities and differences. A comparison-contrast essay organizes one paragraph based on similarities and another based on differences. A comparison-contrast essay can also be arranged with the similarities and differences of individual traits addressed within individual paragraphs. Words such as *however*, *but*, and *nevertheless* help signal a contrast in ideas.

4. *Descriptive* writing structure is designed to appeal to your senses. Much like an artist who constructs a painting, good descriptive writing builds an image in the reader's mind by appealing to the five senses: sight, hearing, taste, touch, and smell. However, overly descriptive writing can become tedious; sparse descriptions can make settings and characters seem flat. Good authors strike a balance by applying descriptions only to passages, characters, and settings that are integral to the plot.

5. Passages that use the *cause and effect* structure are simply asking *why* by demonstrating some type of connection between ideas. Words such as *if*, *since*, *because*, *then*, or *consequently* indicate relationship. By switching the order of a complex sentence, the writer can rearrange the emphasis on different clauses. Saying *If Sheryl is late, we'll miss the dance* is different from saying *We'll miss the dance if Sheryl is late*. One emphasizes Sheryl's tardiness while the other emphasizes missing the dance. Paragraphs can also be arranged in a cause and effect format. Since the format — before and after — is sequential, it is useful when authors wish to discuss the impact of choices. Researchers often apply this paragraph structure to the scientific method.

Point of View

Point of view is an important writing device to consider. In fiction writing, point of view refers to who tells the story or from whose perspective readers are observing as they read. In non-fiction writing, the *point of view* refers to whether the author refers to himself/herself, his/her readers, or chooses not to refer to either. Whether fiction or nonfiction, the author will carefully consider the impact the perspective will have on the purpose and main point of the writing.

- *First-person point of view*: The story is told from the writer's perspective. In fiction, this would mean that the main character is also the narrator. First-person point of view is easily recognized by the use of personal pronouns such as *I, me, we, us, our, my*, and *myself*.

- *Third-person point of view*: In a more formal essay, this would be an appropriate perspective because the focus should be on the subject matter, not the writer or the reader. Third-person point of view is recognized by the use of the pronouns *he, she, they*, and *it*. In fiction writing, third person point of view has a few variations.

    o *Third-person limited* point of view refers to a story told by a narrator who has access to the thoughts and feelings of just one character.

    o In *third-person omniscient* point of view, the narrator has access to the thoughts and feelings of all the characters.

- o In *third-person objective* point of view, the narrator is like a fly on the wall and can see and hear what the characters do and say, but does not have access to their thoughts and feelings.

- *Second-person point of view*: This point of view isn't commonly used in fiction or non-fiction writing because it directly addresses the reader using the pronouns *you*, *your*, and *yourself*. Second-person perspective is more appropriate in direct communication, such as business letters or emails.

Point of View	Pronouns Used
First person	I, me, we, us, our, my, myself
Second person	You, your, yourself
Third person	He, she, it, they

Main Ideas and Supporting Details

Topics and main ideas are critical parts of writing. The *topic* is the subject matter of the piece. An example of a topic would be *global warming*.

The main idea is what the writer wants to say about that topic. A writer may make the point that global warming is a growing problem that must be addressed in order to save the planet. Therefore, the topic is global warming, and the main idea is that it's *a serious problem needing to be addressed*. The topic can be expressed in a word or two, but the main idea should be a complete thought.

An author will likely identify the topic immediately within the title or the first sentence of a passage. The main idea is usually presented in the introduction. In a single passage, the main idea may be identified in the first or last sentence, but it will most likely be directly stated and easily recognized by the reader. Because it is not always stated immediately in a passage, it's important to carefully read the entire passage to identify the main idea.

The main idea should not be confused with the thesis statement. A *thesis statement* is a clear statement of the writer's specific stance and can often be found in the introduction of a non-fiction piece. The thesis is a specific sentence (or two) that offers the direction and focus of the discussion.

In order to illustrate the main idea, a writer will use *supporting details*, the details that provide evidence or examples to help make a point. Supporting details often appear in the form of quotations, paraphrasing, or analysis. Authors should connect details and analysis to the main point.

For example, in the example of global warming, where the author's main idea is to show the seriousness of this growing problem and the need for change, the use of supporting details in this piece would be critical in effectively making that point. Supporting details used here might include *statistics* on an increase in global temperatures and *studies* showing the impact of global warming on the planet. The author could also include *projections* for future climate change in order to illustrate potential lasting effects of global warming.

It's important to evaluate the author's supporting details to be sure that they are credible, provide evidence of the author's point, and directly support the main idea. Though shocking statistics grab readers' attention, their use could be ineffective information in the piece. Details like this are crucial to understanding the passage and evaluating how well the author presents his or her argument and evidence.

Also remember that when most authors write, they want to make a point or send a message. This point or message of a text is known as the theme. Authors may state themes explicitly, like in *Aesop's Fables*. More often, especially in modern literature, readers must infer the theme based on text details. Usually after carefully reading and analyzing an entire text, the theme emerges. Typically, the longer the piece, the more themes you will encounter, though often one theme dominates the rest, as evidenced by the author's purposeful revisiting of it throughout the passage.

Evaluating a Passage

Determining conclusions requires being an active reader, as a reader must make a prediction and analyze facts to identify a conclusion. There are a few ways to determine a logical conclusion, but careful reading is the most important. It's helpful to read a passage a few times, noting details that seem important to the piece. A reader should also identify key words in a passage to determine the logical conclusion or determination that flows from the information presented.

Textual evidence within the details helps readers draw a conclusion about a passage. *Textual evidence* refers to information—facts and examples that support the main point. Textual evidence will likely come from outside sources and can be in the form of quoted or paraphrased material. In order to draw a conclusion from evidence, it's important to examine the credibility and validity of that evidence as well as how (and if) it relates to the main idea.

If an author presents a differing opinion or a *counter-argument* in order to refute it, the reader should consider how and why this information is being presented. It is meant to strengthen the original argument and shouldn't be confused with the author's intended conclusion, but it should also be considered in the reader's final evaluation.

Sometimes, authors explicitly state the conclusion they want readers to understand. Alternatively, a conclusion may not be directly stated. In that case, readers must rely on the implications to form a logical conclusion:

> On the way to the bus stop, Michael realized his homework wasn't in his backpack. He ran back to the house to get it and made it back to the bus just in time.

In this example, though it's never explicitly stated, it can be inferred that Michael is a student on his way to school in the morning. When forming a conclusion from implied information, it's important to read the text carefully to find several pieces of evidence in the text to support the conclusion.

Summarizing is an effective way to draw a conclusion from a passage. A summary is a shortened version of the original text, written by the reader in his/her own words. Focusing on the main points of the original text and including only the relevant details can help readers reach a conclusion. It's important to retain the original meaning of the passage.

Like summarizing, *paraphrasing* can also help a reader fully understand different parts of a text. Paraphrasing calls for the reader to take a small part of the passage and list or describe its main points. Paraphrasing is more than rewording the original passage, though. It should be written in the reader's own words, while still retaining the meaning of the original source. This will indicate an understanding of the original source, yet still help the reader expand on his/her interpretation.

Readers should pay attention to the *sequence*, or the order in which details are laid out in the text, as this can be important to understanding its meaning as a whole. Writers will often use transitional words to help the reader understand the order of events and to stay on track. Words like *next, then, after,* and *finally* show that the order of events is important to the author. In some cases, the author omits these transitional words, and the sequence is implied. Authors may even purposely present the information out of order to make an impact or have an effect on the reader. An example might be when a narrative writer uses *flashback* to reveal information.

Responding to a Passage

There are a few ways for readers to engage actively with the text, such as making inferences and predictions. An *inference* refers to a point that is implied (as opposed to directly-stated) by the evidence presented:

> Bradley packed up all of the items from his desk in a box and said goodbye to his coworkers for the last time.

From this sentence, though it is not directly stated, readers can infer that Bradley is leaving his job. It's necessary to use inference in order to draw conclusions about the meaning of a passage. Authors make implications through character dialogue, thoughts, effects on others, actions, and looks. Like in life, readers must assemble all the clues to form a complete picture.

When making an inference about a passage, it's important to rely only on the information that is provided in the text itself. This helps readers ensure that their conclusions are valid.

Readers will also find themselves making predictions when reading a passage or paragraph. *Predictions* are guesses about what's going to happen next. Readers can use prior knowledge to help make accurate predictions. Prior knowledge is best utilized when readers make links between the current text, previously read texts, and life experiences. Some texts use suspense and foreshadowing to captivate readers:

A cat darted across the street just as the car came careening around the curve.

One unfortunate prediction might be that the car will hit the cat. Of course, predictions aren't always accurate, so it's important to read carefully to the end of the text to determine the accuracy of predictions.

Critical Thinking Skills

It's important to read any piece of writing critically. The goal is to discover the point and purpose of what the author is writing about through analysis. It's also crucial to establish the point or stance the author has taken on the topic of the piece. After determining the author's perspective, readers can then more effectively develop their own viewpoints on the subject of the piece.

It is important to distinguish between *fact and opinion* when reading a piece of writing. A fact is information that can be proven true. If information can be disproved, it is not a fact. For example, water freezes at or below thirty-two degrees Fahrenheit. An argument stating that water freezes at seventy degrees Fahrenheit cannot be supported by data, and is therefore not a fact. Facts tend to be associated with science, mathematics, and statistics. Opinions are information open to debate. Opinions are often tied to subjective concepts like equality, morals, and rights. They can also be controversial. An affirmative argument for a position—such as gun control—can be just as effective as an opposing argument against it.

Authors often use words like *think, feel, believe,* or *in my opinion* when expressing opinion, but these words won't always appear in an opinion piece, especially if it is formally written. An author's opinion may be backed up by facts, which gives it more credibility, but that opinion should not be taken as fact. A critical reader should be suspect of an author's opinion, especially if it is only supported by other opinions.

Fact	Opinion
There are 9 innings in a game of baseball.	Baseball games run too long.
Abraham Lincoln was assassinated on April 14, 1865.	Abraham Lincoln should never have been assassinated.
McDonalds has stores in 118 countries.	McDonalds has the best hamburgers.

Critical readers examine the facts used to support an author's argument. They check the facts against other sources to be sure those facts are correct. They also check the validity of the sources used to be sure those sources are credible, academic, and/or peer- reviewed. Consider that when an author uses another person's opinion to support his or her argument, even if it is an expert's opinion, it is still only an opinion and should not be taken as fact. A strong argument uses valid, measurable facts to support ideas. Even then, the reader may disagree with the argument as it may be rooted in his or her personal beliefs.

An authoritative argument may use the facts to sway the reader. In the example of global warming, many experts differ in their opinions of what alternative fuels can be used to aid in offsetting it. Because of this, a writer may choose to only use the information and expert opinion that supports his or her viewpoint.

If the argument is that wind energy is the best solution, the author will use facts that support this idea. That same author may leave out relevant facts on solar energy. The way the author uses facts can influence the reader, so it's important to consider the facts being used, how those facts are being presented, and what information might be left out.

Critical readers should also look for errors in the argument such as logical fallacies and bias. A *logical fallacy* is a flaw in the logic used to make the argument. Logical fallacies include slippery slope, straw man, and begging the question. Authors can also reflect *bias* if they ignore an opposing viewpoint or present their side in an unbalanced way. A strong argument considers the opposition and finds a way to refute it. Critical readers should look for an unfair or one-sided presentation of the argument and be skeptical, as a bias may be present. Even if this bias is unintentional, if it exists in the writing, the reader should be wary of the validity of the argument.

Readers should also look for the use of *stereotypes,* which refer to specific groups. Stereotypes are often negative connotations about a person or place and should always be avoided. When a critical reader finds stereotypes in a piece of writing, they should immediately be critical of the argument and consider the validity of anything the author presents. Stereotypes reveal a flaw in the writer's thinking and may suggest a lack of knowledge or understanding about the subject.

Practice Questions

Directions for questions 1–10

Read the statement or passage and then choose the best answer to the question. Answer the question based on what is stated or implied in the statement or passage.

1. While scientists aren't entirely certain why tornadoes form, they have some clues into the process. Tornadoes are dangerous funnel clouds that occur during a large thunderstorm. When warm, humid air near the ground meets cold, dry air from above, a column of the warm air can be drawn up into the clouds. Winds at different altitudes blowing at different speeds make the column of air rotate. As the spinning column of air picks up speed, a funnel cloud is formed. This funnel cloud moves rapidly and haphazardly. Rain and hail inside the cloud cause it to touch down, creating a tornado. Tornadoes move in a rapid and unpredictable pattern, making them extremely destructive and dangerous. Scientists continue to study tornadoes to improve radar detection and warning times.

The main purpose of this passage is to:
    a. Show why tornadoes are dangerous
    b. Explain how a tornado forms
    c. Compare thunderstorms to tornadoes
    d. Explain what to do in the event of a tornado

2. There are two major kinds of cameras on the market right now for amateur photographers. Camera enthusiasts can either purchase a digital single-lens reflex camera (DSLR) camera or a compact system camera (CSC). The main difference between a DSLR and a CSC is that the DSLR has a full-sized sensor, which means it fits in a much larger body. The CSC uses a mirrorless system, which makes for a lighter, smaller camera. While both take quality pictures, the DSLR generally has better picture quality due to the larger sensor. CSCs still take very good quality pictures and are more convenient to carry than a DSLR. This makes the CSC an ideal choice for the amateur photographer looking to step up from a point-and-shoot camera.

The main difference between the DSLR and CSC is:
    a. The picture quality is better in the DSLR.
    b. The CSC is less expensive than the DSLR.
    c. The DSLR is a better choice for amateur photographers.
    d. The DSLR's larger sensor makes it a bigger camera than the CSC.

3. When selecting a career path, it's important to explore the various options available. Many students entering college may shy away from a major because they don't know much about it. For example, many students won't opt for a career as an actuary, because they aren't exactly sure what it entails. They would be missing out on a career that is very lucrative and in high demand. Actuaries work in the insurance field and assess risks and premiums. The average salary of an actuary is $100,000 per year. Another career option students may avoid, due to lack of knowledge of the field, is a hospitalist. This is a physician that specializes in the care of patients in a hospital, as opposed to those seen in private practices. The average salary of a hospitalist is upwards of $200,000. It pays to do some digging and find out more about these lesser-known career fields.

An actuary is:
   a. A doctor who works in a hospital
   b. The same as a hospitalist
   c. An insurance agent who works in a hospital
   d. A person who assesses insurance risks and premiums

4. Many people are unsure of exactly how the digestive system works. Digestion begins in the mouth where teeth grind up food and saliva breaks it down, making it easier for the body to absorb. Next, the food moves to the esophagus, and it is pushed into the stomach. The stomach is where food is stored and broken down further by acids and digestive enzymes, preparing it for passage into the intestines. The small intestine is where the nutrients are taken from food and passed into the blood stream. Other essential organs like the liver, gall bladder, and pancreas aid the stomach in breaking down food and absorbing nutrients. Finally, food waste is passed into the large intestine where it is eliminated by the body.

The purpose of this passage is to:
   a. Explain how the liver works.
   b. Show why it is important to eat healthy foods
   c. Explain how the digestive system works
   d. Show how nutrients are absorbed by the small intestine

5. Hard water occurs when rainwater mixes with minerals from rock and soil. Hard water has a high mineral count, including calcium and magnesium. The mineral deposits from hard water can stain hard surfaces in bathrooms and kitchens as well as clog pipes. Hard water can stain dishes, ruin clothes, and reduce the life of any appliances it touches, such as hot water heaters, washing machines, and humidifiers.

One solution is to install a water softener to reduce the mineral content of water, but this can be costly. Running vinegar through pipes and appliances and using vinegar to clean hard surfaces can also help with mineral deposits.

From this passage, it can be concluded that:
   a. Hard water can cause a lot of problems for homeowners.
   b. Calcium is good for pipes and hard surfaces.
   c. Water softeners are easy to install.
   d. Vinegar is the only solution to hard water problems.

6. Osteoporosis is a medical condition that occurs when the body loses bone or makes too little bone. This can lead to brittle, fragile bones that easily break. Bones are already porous, and when osteoporosis sets in, the spaces in bones become much larger, causing them to weaken. Both men and

women can contract osteoporosis, though it is most common in women over age 50. Loss of bone can be silent and progressive, so it is important to be proactive in prevention of the disease.

The main purpose of this passage is to:
    a. Discuss some of the ways people contract osteoporosis
    b. Describe different treatment options for those with osteoporosis
    c. Explain how to prevent osteoporosis
    d. Define osteoporosis

7. Vacationers looking for a perfect experience should opt out of Disney parks and try a trip on Disney Cruise Lines. While a park offers rides, characters, and show experiences, it also includes long lines, often very hot weather, and enormous crowds. A Disney Cruise, on the other hand, is a relaxing, luxurious vacation that includes many of the same experiences as the parks, minus the crowds and lines. The cruise has top-notch food, maid service, water slides, multiple pools, Broadway-quality shows, and daily character experiences for kids. There are also many activities, such as bingo, trivia contests, and dance parties that can entertain guests of all ages. The cruise even stops at Disney's private island for a beach barbecue with characters, waterslides, and water sports. Those looking for the Disney experience without the hassle should book a Disney cruise.

The main purpose of this passage is to:
    a. Explain how to book a Disney cruise
    b. Show what Disney parks have to offer
    c. Show why Disney parks are expensive
    d. Compare Disney parks to the Disney cruise

8. Coaches of kids' sports teams are increasingly concerned about the behavior of parents at games. Parents are screaming and cursing at coaches, officials, players, and other parents. Physical fights have even broken out at games. Parents need to be reminded that coaches are volunteers, giving up their time and energy to help kids develop in their chosen sport. The goal of kids' sports teams is to learn and develop skills, but it's also to have fun. When parents are out of control at games and practices, it takes the fun out of the sport.

From this passage, it can be concluded that:
    a. Coaches are modeling good behavior for kids.
    b. Organized sports are not good for kids.
    c. Parents' behavior at their kids' games needs to change.
    d. Parents and coaches need to work together.

9. As summer approaches, drowning incidents will increase. Drowning happens very quickly and silently. Most people assume that drowning is easy to spot, but a person who is drowning doesn't make noise or wave his arms. Instead, he will have his head back and his mouth open, with just his face out of the water. A person who is truly in danger of drowning is not able to wave his arms in the air or move much at all. Recognizing these signs of drowning can prevent tragedy.

The main purpose of this passage is to:
    a. Explain the dangers of swimming
    b. Show how to identify the signs of drowning
    c. Explain how to be a lifeguard
    d. Compare the signs of drowning

10. Technology has been invading cars for the last several years, but there are some new high tech trends that are pretty amazing. It is now standard in many car models to have a rear-view camera, hands-free phone and text, and a touch screen digital display. Music can be streamed from a paired cell phone, and some displays can even be programmed with a personal photo. Sensors beep to indicate there is something in the driver's path when reversing and changing lanes. Rain-sensing windshield wipers and lights are automatic, leaving the driver with little to do but watch the road and enjoy the ride. The next wave of technology will include cars that automatically parallel park, and a self-driving car is on the horizon. These technological advances make it a good time to be a driver.

It can be concluded from this paragraph that:
    a. Technology will continue to influence how cars are made.
    b. Windshield wipers and lights are always automatic.
    c. It is standard to have a rear-view camera in all cars.
    d. Technology has reached its peak in cars.

Directions for questions 11–20

For the questions that follow, two underlined sentences are followed by a question or statement. Read the sentences, then choose the best answer to the question or the best completion of the statement.

11. The NBA draft process is based on a lottery system among the teams who did not make the playoffs in the previous season to determine draft order. Only the top three draft picks are determined by the lottery.

What does the *second sentence* do?
    a. It contradicts the first.
    b. It supports the first.
    c. It restates information from the first.
    d. It offers a solution.

12. While many people use multiple social media sites, Facebook remains the most popular with more than one billion users. Instagram is rising in popularity and, with 100 million users, is now the most-used social media site.

What does the *second sentence* do?
    a. It expands on the first.
    b. It contradicts the first.
    c. It supports the first.
    d. It proposes a solution.

13. There are eight different phases of the moon, from new moon to new moon. One of the eight different moon phases is first quarter, commonly called a half moon.

What does the *second sentence* do?
    a. It provides an example.
    b. It contradicts the first.
    c. It states an effect.
    d. It offers a solution.

14. The terror attacks of September 11, 2001 have had many lasting effects on the United States. The Department of Homeland Security was created in late September 2001 in response to the terror attacks and became an official cabinet-level department in November of 2002.

What does the *second sentence* do?
    a. It contradicts the first.
    b. It restates the information from the first.
    c. It states an effect.
    d. It makes a contrast.

15. Annuals are plants that complete the life cycle in a single growing season. Perennials are plants that complete the life cycle in many growing seasons, dying in the winter and coming back each spring.

What does the *second sentence* do?
    a. It makes a contrast.
    b. It disputes the first sentence.
    c. It provides an example.
    d. It states an effect.

16. Personal computers can be subject to viruses and malware, which can lead to slow performance, loss of files, and overheating. Antivirus software is often sold along with a new PC to protect against viruses and malware.

What does the *second sentence* do?
    a. It makes a contrast.
    b. It provides an example.
    c. It restates the information from the first.
    d. It offers a solution.

17. Many companies tout their chicken as cage-free because the chickens are not confined to small wire cages. However, cage-free chickens are often crammed into buildings with thousands of other birds and never go outside in their short lifetime.

What does the *second sentence* do?
    a. It offers a solution.
    b. It provides an example.
    c. It disputes the first sentence.
    d. It states an effect.

18. Common core standards do not include the instruction of cursive handwriting. The next generation of students will not be able to read or write cursive handwriting.

What does the *second sentence* do?
    a. It offers a solution.
    b. It states an effect.
    c. It contradicts the first sentence.
    d. It restates the first sentence.

19. Air travel has changed significantly in the last ten years. Airlines are now offering pay-as-you-go perks, including no baggage fees, seat selection, and food and drinks on the flight to keep costs low.

What does the *second sentence* do?
    a. It states effects.
    b. It provides examples.
    c. It disputes the first sentence.
    d. It offers solutions.

20. Many people are unaware that fragrances and other chemicals in their favorite products are causing skin reactions and allergies. Surprisingly, many popular products contain ingredients that can cause skin allergies.

What does the *second sentence* do?
    a. It restates the first sentence.
    b. It provides examples.
    c. It contradicts the first sentence.
    d. It provides solutions.

Answer Explanations

1. B: The main point of this passage is to show how a tornado forms. Choice A is off base because while the passage does mention that tornadoes are dangerous, it is not the main focus of the passage. While thunderstorms are mentioned, they are not compared to tornadoes, so Choice C is incorrect. Choice D is incorrect because the passage does not discuss what to do in the event of a tornado.

2. D: The passage directly states that the larger sensor is the main difference between the two cameras. Choices A and B may be true, but these answers do not identify the major difference between the two cameras. Choice C states the opposite of what the paragraph suggests is the best option for amateur photographers, so it is incorrect.

3. D: An actuary assesses risks and sets insurance premiums. While an actuary does work in insurance, the passage does not suggest that actuaries have any affiliation with hospitalists or working in a hospital, so all other choices are incorrect.

4. C: The purpose of this passage is to explain how the digestive system works. Choice A focuses only on the liver, which is a small part of the process and not the focus of the paragraph. Choice B is off-track because the passage does not mention healthy foods. Choice D only focuses on one part of the digestive system.

5. A: The passage focuses mainly on the problems of hard water. Choice B is incorrect because calcium is not good for pipes and hard surfaces. The passage does not say anything about whether water softeners are easy to install, so C is incorrect. D is also incorrect because the passage does offer other solutions besides vinegar.

6. D: The main point of this passage is to define osteoporosis. Choice A is incorrect because the passage does not list ways that people contract osteoporosis. Choice B is incorrect because the passage does not mention any treatment options. While the passage does briefly mention prevention, it does not explain how, so Choice C is incorrect.

7. D: The passage compares Disney cruises with Disney parks. It does not discuss how to book a cruise, so Choice A is incorrect. Choice B is incorrect because though the passage does mention some of the park attractions, it is not the main point. The passage does not mention the cost of either option, so Choice C is incorrect.

8. C: The main point of this paragraph is that parents need to change their poor behavior at their kids' sporting events. Choice A is incorrect because the coaches' behavior is not mentioned in the paragraph. B suggests that sports are bad for kids, when the paragraph is about parents' behavior, so it is incorrect. While Choice D may be true, it offers a specific solution to the problem, which the paragraph does not discuss.

9. B: The point of this passage is to show what drowning looks like. Choice A is incorrect because while drowning is a danger of swimming, the passage doesn't include any other dangers. The passage is not intended for lifeguards specifically, but for a general audience, so Choice C is incorrect. There are a few signs of drowning, but the passage does not compare them; thus, Choice D is incorrect.

10. A: The passage discusses recent technological advances in cars and suggests that this trend will continue in the future with self-driving cars. Choice *B* and *C* are not true, so these are both incorrect. Choice *D* is also incorrect because the passage suggests continuing growth in technology, not a peak.

11. B: The information in the second sentence further explains the draft process and thus supports the first sentence. It does not contradict the first sentence, so *A* is incorrect. Choice *C* and *D* are incorrect because the second sentence does not restate or offer a solution to the first.

12. B: The first sentence identifies Facebook as the most popular social media site with 1 billion users. The second sentence states that Instagram only has 100 million users, but is the most used. This contradicts the original sentence, so all other answers are incorrect.

13. A: The first sentence states that there are eight phases to the moon cycle. The second sentence discusses first quarter, which is one of the phases of the moon. Therefore, the second sentence provides an example of the first sentence.

14. C: The first sentence discusses the effects of the terror attacks of September 11, 2001. The second sentence states that the Department of Homeland Security was created in response to the terror attacks, so it states an effect of the first sentence.

15. A: The first sentence describes the life cycle of annuals. The second sentence describes the life cycle of perennials, making a contrast between the way annuals grow and the way perennials grow.

16. D: The first sentence describes how viruses can affect a PC. The second sentence offers a solution to the problem of viruses and malware on a PC.

17. C: The first sentence describes cage-free chickens as not being confined to a cage, suggesting they are treated humanely. The second sentence disputes the first sentence, showing that cage-free chickens are inhumanely confined to a larger area with many other chickens, never seeing the outdoors.

18. B: The first sentence states that schools are no longer teaching cursive handwriting. The second sentence shows that as an effect of the first sentence, students will no longer be able to read or write cursive handwriting.

19. B: The first sentence states that air travel has changed in the last decade. The second sentence provides examples of the changes that have occurred.

20. A: The first sentence discusses how fragrances and other chemicals in products can cause skin reactions. The second sentence states that many products contain ingredients that cause skin allergies, restating the same information from the first sentence.

Sentence Skills Test

Sentence Correction

In this section of the test, each example contains a sentence with an <u>underlined</u> portion. The multiple choice answers will offer reworded versions of the underlined part of the sentence. The first answer choice will repeat the original sentence, and the others will offer different options for how to re-word the sentence.

The goal of these questions is to test an individual's ability to recognize the most effective way to express something, using correct grammar, word choice, and sentence structure. The correct answer will be grammatically-correct, with a clear, concise flow.

Construction Shift

These multiple-choice questions ask the test-taker to rewrite the original sentence so that it is more correct in terms of grammar, word choice, and sentence structure. These questions will provide the beginning of the new sentence and then offer four options for ending the sentence. The goal is to select the answer choice that makes the best structured sentence, while retaining the meaning of the original sentence. In most cases, when the sentence is rewritten, it will entail changing a dependent clause to an independent clause, or an independent clause to a dependent clause.

Answers should be chosen carefully, ensuring that they adhere to the rules of grammar and standard English. The best choice will be the one that is correct, concise, and clear, while also retaining the meaning of the original sentence.

A helpful strategy is to predict the sentence ending before looking at the answer choices. This approach helps in selecting the one that makes the most sense. Reading the answer choices first might be confusing and make the choice more difficult. In these questions, the simplest answer is often the best answer.

Types of Sentences

There isn't an overabundance of absolutes in grammar, but here is one: every sentence in the English language falls into one of four categories.

- Declarative: a simple statement that ends with a period

    The price of milk per gallon is the same as the price of gasoline.

- Imperative: a command, instruction, or request that ends with a period

    Buy milk when you stop to fill up your car with gas.

- Interrogative: a question that ends with a question mark

    Will you buy the milk?

- Exclamatory: a statement or command that expresses emotions like anger, urgency, or surprise and ends with an exclamation mark

> Buy the milk now!

Declarative sentences are the most common type, probably because they are comprised of the most general content, without any of the bells and whistles that the other three types contain. They are, simply, declarations or statements of any degree of seriousness, importance, or information.

Imperative sentences often seem to be missing a subject. The subject is there, though; it is just not visible or audible because it is *implied*. Look at the imperative example sentence.

> Buy the milk when you fill up your car with gas.

You is the implied subject, the one to whom the command is issued. This is sometimes called *the understood you* because it is understood that *you* is the subject of the sentence.

Interrogative sentences—those that ask questions—are defined as such from the idea of the word *interrogation*, the action of questions being asked of suspects by investigators. Although that is serious business, interrogative sentences apply to all kinds of questions.

To exclaim is at the root of *exclamatory* sentences. These are made with strong emotions behind them. The only technical difference between a declarative or imperative sentence and an exclamatory one is the exclamation mark at the end. The example declarative and imperative sentences can both become an exclamatory one simply by putting an exclamation mark at the end of the sentences.

> The price of milk per gallon is the same as the price of gasoline!
> Buy milk when you stop to fill up your car with gas!

After all, someone might be really excited by the price of gas or milk, or they could be mad at the person that will be buying the milk! However, as stated before, exclamation marks in abundance defeat their own purpose! After a while, they begin to cause fatigue! When used only for their intended purpose, they can have their expected and desired effect.

Parts of Speech

Nouns
A noun is a person, place, thing ,or idea. All nouns fit into one of two types, common or proper.

A *common noun* is a word that identifies any of a class of people, places, or things. Examples include numbers, objects, animals, feelings, concepts, qualities, and actions. *A, an,* or *the* usually precedes the common noun. These parts of speech are called *articles*. Here are some examples of sentences using nouns preceded by articles.

> *A* building is under construction.
> *The* girl would like to move to *the* city.

A *proper noun* (also called a *proper name*) is used for the specific name of an individual person, place, or organization. The first letter in a proper noun is capitalized. "My name is *Mary*." "I work for *Walmart*."

Nouns sometimes serve as adjectives (which themselves describe nouns), such as "hockey player" and "state government."

An abstract noun is an idea, state, or quality. It is something that can't be touched, such as happiness, courage, evil, or humor.

A concrete noun is something that can be experienced through the senses (touch, taste, hear, smell, see). Examples of concrete nouns are birds, skateboard, pie, and car.

A collective noun refers to a collection of people, places, or things that act as one. Examples of collective nouns are as follows: team, class, jury, family, audience, and flock.

Pronouns

A word used in place of a noun is known as a *pronoun*. Pronouns are words like *I, mine, hers,* and *us*.

Pronouns can be split into different classifications (seen below) which make them easier to learn; however, it's not important to memorize the classifications.

- Personal pronouns: refer to people
- first person: we, I, our, mine
- second person: you, yours
- third person: he, them
- Possessive pronouns: demonstrate ownership (mine, my, his, yours)
- Interrogative pronouns: ask questions (what, which, who, whom, whose)
- Relative pronouns: include the five interrogative pronouns and others that are relative (whoever, whomever, that, when, where)
- Demonstrative pronouns: replace something specific (this, that, those, these)
- Reciprocal pronouns: indicate something was done or given in return (each other, one another)
- Indefinite pronouns: have a nonspecific status (anybody, whoever, someone, everybody, somebody)

Indefinite pronouns such as *anybody, whoever, someone, everybody*, and *somebody* command a singular verb form, but others such as *all, none,* and *some* could require a singular or plural verb form.

Antecedents

An *antecedent* is the noun to which a pronoun refers; it needs to be written or spoken before the pronoun is used. For many pronouns, antecedents are imperative for clarity. In particular, many of the personal, possessive, and demonstrative pronouns need antecedents. Otherwise, it would be unclear who or what someone is referring to when they use a pronoun like *he* or *this*.

Pronoun reference means that the pronoun should refer clearly to one, clear, unmistakable noun (the antecedent).

Pronoun-antecedent agreement refers to the need for the antecedent and the corresponding pronoun to agree in gender, person, and number. Here are some examples:

The *kidneys* (plural antecedent) are part of the urinary system. *They* (plural pronoun) serve several roles."

The kidneys are part of the *urinary system* (singular antecedent). *It* (singular pronoun) is also known as the renal system.

Pronoun Cases

The subjective pronouns —*I, you, he/she/it, we, they,* and *who*—are the subjects of the sentence.

>   Example: *They* have a new house.

The objective pronouns—*me, you* (*singular*), *him/her, us, them,* and *whom*—are used when something is being done for or given to someone; they are objects of the action.

>   Example: The teacher has an apple for *us.*

The possessive pronouns—*mine, my, your, yours, his, hers, its, their, theirs, our,* and *ours*—are used to denote that something (or someone) belongs to someone (or something).

>   Example: It's *their* chocolate cake.
>   Even Better Example: It's *my* chocolate cake!

One of the greatest challenges and worst abuses of pronouns concerns *who* and *whom.* Just knowing the following rule can eliminate confusion. *Who* is a subjective-case pronoun used only as a subject or subject complement. *Whom* is only objective-case and, therefore, the object of the verb or preposition.

Hint: When using *who* or *whom,* think of whether someone would say *he* or *him.* If the answer is *he,* use *who.* If the answer is *him,* use *whom.* This trick is easy to remember because *he* and *who* both end in vowels, and *him* and *whom* both end in the letter *M.*

Verbs

The *verb* is the part of speech that describes an action, state of being, or occurrence.

A *verb* forms the main part of a predicate of a sentence. This means that the verb explains what the noun (which will be discussed shortly) is doing. A simple example is *time flies.* The verb *flies* explains what the action of the noun, *time,* is doing. This example is a *main* verb.

Helping (*auxiliary*) verbs are words like *have, do, be, can, may, should, must,* and *will.* "I *should* go to the store." Helping verbs assist main verbs in expressing tense, ability, possibility, permission, or obligation.

Particles are minor function words like *not, in, out, up,* or *down* that become part of the verb itself. "I might *not.*"

Participles are words formed from verbs that are often used to modify a noun, noun phrase, verb, or verb phrase.

>   The *running* teenager collided with the cyclist.

Participles can also create compound verb forms.

>   He is *speaking.*

Verbs have five basic forms: the *base* form, the *-s* form, the *-ing* form, the *past* form, and the *past participle* form.

The *past* forms are either *regular* (*love/loved; hate/hated*) or *irregular* because they don't end by adding the common past tense suffix "-ed" (*go/went; fall/fell; set/set*).

<u>Verb Forms</u>
Shifting verb forms entails *conjugation*, which is used to indicate *tense, voice,* or *mood.*

Verb tense is used to show when the action in the sentence took place. There are several different verb tenses, and it is important to know how and when to use them. Some verb tenses can be achieved by changing the form of the verb, while others require the use of helping verbs (e.g., *is, was,* or *has*).

Present tense shows the action is happening currently or is ongoing:

> I walk to work every morning.

> She is stressed about the deadline.

Past tense shows that the action happened in the past or that the state of being is in the past:

> I walked to work yesterday morning.

> She was stressed about the deadline.

Future tense shows that the action will happen in the future or is a future state of being:

> I will walk to work tomorrow morning.

> She will be stressed about the deadline.

Present perfect tense shows action that began in the past, but continues into the present:

> I have walked to work all week.

> She has been stressed about the deadline.

Past perfect tense shows an action was finished before another took place:

> I had walked all week until I sprained my ankle.

> She had been stressed about the deadline until we talked about it.

Future perfect tense shows an action that will be completed at some point in the future:

> By the time the bus arrives, I will have walked to work already.

<u>Voice</u>
Verbs can be in the active or passive voice. When the subject completes the action, the verb is in *active voice*. When the subject receives the action of the sentence, the verb is in *passive voice*.

> Active: Jamie ate the ice cream.

> Passive: The ice cream was eaten by Jamie.

In active voice, the subject (*Jamie*) is the "do-er" of the action (*ate*). In passive voice, the subject *ice cream* receives the action of being eaten.

While passive voice can add variety to writing, active voice is the generally preferred sentence structure.

Mood

Mood is used to show the speaker's feelings about the subject matter. In English, there is *indicative mood, imperative mood,* and *subjective mood.*

Indicative mood is used to state facts, ask questions, or state opinions:

Bob will make the trip next week.

When can Bob make the trip?

Imperative mood is used to state a command or make a request:

Wait in the lobby.

Please call me next week.

Subjunctive mood is used to express a wish, an opinion, or a hope that is contrary to fact:

If I were in charge, none of this would have happened.

Allison wished she could take the exam over again when she saw her score.

Adjectives

Adjectives are words used to modify nouns and pronouns. They can be used alone or in a series and are used to further define or describe the nouns they modify.

Mark made us a delicious, four-course meal.

The words *delicious* and *four-course* are adjectives that describe the kind of meal Mark made.

Articles are also considered adjectives because they help to describe nouns. Articles can be general or specific. The three articles in English are: a, an, and the.

Indefinite articles (a, an) are used to refer to nonspecific nouns. The article *a* proceeds words beginning with consonant sounds, and the article *an* proceeds words beginning with vowel sounds.

A car drove by our house.

An alligator was loose at the zoo.

He has always wanted a ukulele. (The first *u* makes a *y* sound.)

Note that *a* and *an* should only proceed nonspecific nouns that are also singular. If a nonspecific noun is plural, it does not need a preceding article.

Alligators were loose at the zoo.

The *definite article (the)* is used to refer to specific nouns:

The car pulled into our driveway.

Note that *the* should proceed all specific nouns regardless of whether they are singular or plural.

The cars pulled into our driveway.

Comparative adjectives are used to compare nouns. When they are used in this way, they take on positive, comparative, or superlative form.

The *positive* form is the normal form of the adjective:

Alicia is tall.

The *comparative* form shows a comparison between two things:

Alicia is taller than Maria.

Superlative form shows comparison between more than two things:

Alicia is the tallest girl in her class.

Usually, the comparative and superlative can be made by adding –er and –est to the positive form, but some verbs call for the helping verbs *more* or *most*. Other exceptions to the rule include adjectives like *bad*, which uses the comparative *worse* and the superlative *worst*.

An adjective phrase is not a bunch of adjectives strung together, but a group of words that describes a noun or pronoun and, thus, functions as an adjective. *Very ugly* is an adjective phrase; so are *way too fat* and *faster than a speeding bullet.*

Adverbs

Adverbs have more functions than adjectives because they modify or qualify verbs, adjectives, or other adverbs as well as word groups that express a relation of place, time, circumstance, or cause. Therefore, adverbs answer any of the following questions: *How, when, where, why, in what way, how often, how much, in what condition,* and/or *to what degree. How good looking is he? He is <u>very</u> handsome.*

Here are some examples of adverbs for different situations:

- how: quickly
- when: daily
- where: there
- in what way: easily
- how often: often
- how much: much
- in what condition: badly
- what degree: hardly

As one can see, for some reason, many adverbs end in *-ly*.

Adverbs do things like emphasize (*really, simply,* and *so*), amplify (*heartily, completely,* and *positively*), and tone down (*almost, somewhat,* and *mildly*).

Adverbs also come in phrases.

The dog ran as <u>though his life depended on it.</u>

Prepositions

Prepositions are connecting words and, while there are only about 150 of them, they are used more often than any other individual groups of words. They describe relationships between other words. They are placed before a noun or pronoun, forming a phrase that modifies another word in the sentence. *Prepositional phrases* begin with a preposition and end with a noun or pronoun, the *object of the preposition. A pristine lake is <u>near the store</u> and <u>behind the bank</u>.*

Some commonly used prepositions are *about, after, anti, around, as, at, behind, beside, by, for, from, in, into, of, off, on, to,* and *with.*

Complex prepositions, which also come before a noun or pronoun, consist of two or three words such as *according to, in regards to,* and *because of.*

Conjunctions

Conjunctions are vital words that connect words, phrases, thoughts, and ideas. Conjunctions show relationships between components. There are two types:

Coordinating conjunctions are the primary class of conjunctions placed between words, phrases, clauses, and sentences that are of equal grammatical rank; the coordinating conjunctions are *or, and, nor, but, or, yes,* and *so.* A useful memorization trick is to remember that the first letter of these conjunctions collectively spell the word *fanboys.*

> I need to go shopping, *but* I must be careful to leave enough money in the bank.
> She wore a black, red, *and* white shirt.

Subordinating conjunctions are the secondary class of conjunctions. They connect two unequal parts, one *main* (or *independent*) and the other *subordinate* (or *dependent*). I must go to the store *even though* I do not have enough money in the bank.

> *Because* I read the review, I do not want to go to the movie.

Notice that the presence of subordinating conjunctions makes clauses dependent. *I read the movie* is an independent clause, but *because* makes the clause dependent. Thus, it needs an independent clause to complete the sentence.

Interjections

Interjections are words used to express emotion. Examples include *wow, ouch,* and *hooray.* Interjections are often separate from sentences; in those cases, the interjection is directly followed by an exclamation point. In other cases the interjection is included in a sentence and followed by a comma. The punctuation plays a big role in the intensity of the emotion that the interjection is expressing. Using a comma or semicolon indicates less excitement than using an exclamation mark.

Capitalization Rules

Here's a non-exhaustive list of things that should be capitalized.

- the first word of every sentence
- the first word of every line of poetry
- the first letter of proper nouns (World War II)
- holidays (Valentine's Day)
- days of the week and months of the year (Tuesday, March)

- the first word, last word, and all major words in the titles of books, movies, songs, and other creative works (*To Kill a Mockingbird,* note that *a* is lowercase since it's not a major word, but *to* is capitalized since it's the first word of the title.
- titles when preceding a proper noun (President Roberto Gonzales, Aunt Judy)

When simply using a word such as president or secretary, though, the word is not capitalized.

Officers of the new business must include a *president* and *treasurer*.

Seasons—spring, fall, etc.—are not capitalized.

North, *south*, *east*, and *west* are capitalized when referring to regions but are not when being used for directions. In general, if it's preceded by *the* it should be capitalized.

I'm from the South.
I drove south.

End Punctuation

Periods (.) are used to end a sentence that is a statement (*declarative*) or a command (*imperative*). They should not be used in a sentence that asks a question or is an exclamation. Periods are also used in abbreviations, which are shortened versions of words.

- Declarative: The boys refused to go to sleep.
- Imperative: Walk down to the bus stop.
- Abbreviations: Joan Roberts, M.D., Apple Inc., Mrs. Adamson
- If a sentence ends with an abbreviation, it is inappropriate to use two periods. It should end with a single period after the abbreviation.

The chef gathered the ingredients for the pie, which included apples, flour, sugar, etc.

Question marks (?) are used with direct questions (*interrogative*). An *indirect question* can use a period:

Interrogative: When does the next bus arrive?

Indirect Question: I wonder when the next bus arrives.

An *exclamation point (!)* is used to show strong emotion or can be used as an *interjection*. This punctuation should be used sparingly in formal writing situations.

What an amazing shot!

Whoa!

Commas

A *comma* (,) is the punctuation mark that signifies a pause—breath—between parts of a sentence. It denotes a break of flow. Proper comma usage helps readers understand the writer's intended emphasis of ideas.

In a complex sentence—one that contains a subordinate (dependent) clause or clauses—separate the clauses with commas.

> I will not pay for the steak, *because I don't have that much money.*

First, see how the purpose of each comma usage is to designate an interruption in flow. Then, notice how the last clause is dependent because it requires the earlier independent clauses to make sense.

Use a comma on both sides of an interrupting phrase.

> I will pay for the ice cream, *chocolate and vanilla,* and I will eat it all myself.

The words forming the phrase in italics are nonessential (extra) information. To determine if a phrase is nonessential, try reading the sentence without the phrase and see if it's still coherent.

A comma is not necessary in this next sentence because no interruption—nonessential or extra information—has occurred. Read sentences aloud when uncertain.

I will pay for his chocolate and vanilla ice cream and I will eat it all myself.

If the nonessential phrase comes at the beginning of a sentence, a comma should only go at the end of the phrase. If the phrase comes at the end of a sentence, a comma should only go at the beginning of the phrase.

Other types of interruptions include the following:

- interjections: Oh no, I am not going.
- abbreviations: Barry Potter, M.D., specializes in heart disorders.
- direct addresses: Yes, Claudia, I am tired and going to bed.
- parenthetical phrases: His wife, lovely as she was, was not helpful.
- transitional phrases: Also, it is not possible.

The second comma in the following sentence is called an Oxford comma.

> I will pay for ice cream, syrup, and pop.

It is a comma used after the second-to-last item in a series of three or more items. It comes before the word *or* or *and*. Not everyone uses the Oxford comma; it is optional, but many believe it is needed. The comma functions as a tool to reduce confusion in writing. So, if omitting the Oxford comma would cause confusion, then it's best to include it.

Commas are used in math to mark the place of thousands in numerals, breaking them up so they are easier to read. Other uses for commas are in dates (*March 19, 2016*), letter greetings (*Dear Sally,*), and in between cities and states (*Louisville, KY*).

Semicolons

A *semicolon (;)* is used to connect ideas in a sentence in some way. There are three main ways to use semicolons.

Link two independent clauses without the use of a coordinating conjunction:

> I was late for work again; I'm definitely going to get fired.

Link two independent clauses with a transitional word:

> The songs were all easy to play; therefore, he didn't need to spend too much time practicing.

Between items in a series that are already separated by commas or if necessary to separate lengthy items in a list:

> Starbucks has locations in Media, PA; Swarthmore, PA; and Morton, PA.

> Several classroom management issues presented in the study: the advent of a poor teacher persona in the context of voice, dress, and style; teacher follow-through from the beginning of the school year to the end; and the depth of administrative support, including ISS and OSS protocol.

Colons

A *colon* is used after an independent clause to present an explanation or draw attention to what comes next in the sentence. There are several uses.

Explanations of ideas:

> They soon learned the hardest part about having a new baby: sleep deprivation.

Lists of items:

> Shari picked up all the supplies she would need for the party: cups, plates, napkins, balloons, streamers, and party favors.

Time, subtitles, general salutations:

> The time is 7:15.

> I read a book entitled *Pluto: A Planet No More*.

> To whom it may concern:

Parentheses and Dashes

Parentheses are half-round brackets that look like this: ( ). They set off a word, phrase, or sentence that is an afterthought, explanation, or side note relevant to the surrounding text but not essential. A pair of commas is often used to set off this sort of information, but parentheses are generally used for information that would not fit well within a sentence or that the writer deems not important enough to be structurally part of the sentence.

> The picture of the heart (see above) shows the major parts you should memorize.
> Mount Everest is one of three mountains in the world that are over 28,000 feet high (K2 and Kanchenjunga are the other two).

See how the sentences above are complete without the parenthetical statements? In the first example, *see above* would not have fit well within the flow of the sentence. The second parenthetical statement could have been a separate sentence, but the writer deemed the information not pertinent to the topic.

The dash (—) is a mark longer than a hyphen used as a punctuation mark in sentences and to set apart a relevant thought. Even after plucking out the line separated by the dash marks, the sentence will be intact and make sense.

> Looking out the airplane window at the landmarks—Lake Clarke, Thompson Community College, and the bridge—she couldn't help but feel excited to be home.

The dashes use is similar to that of parentheses or a pair of commas. So, what's the difference? Many believe that using dashes makes the clause within them stand out while using parentheses is subtler. It's advised to not use dashes when commas could be used instead.

Ellipses

An *ellipsis* (...) consists of three handy little dots that can speak volumes on behalf of irrelevant material. Writers use them in place of a word(s), line, phrase, list contents, or paragraph that might just as easily have been omitted from a passage of writing. This can be done to save space or to focus only on the specifically relevant material.

> Exercise is good for some unexpected reasons. Watkins writes, "Exercise has many benefits such as ...reducing cancer risk."

In the example above, the ellipsis takes the place of the other benefits of exercise that are more expected.

The ellipsis may also be used to show a pause in sentence flow.

> "I'm wondering...how this could happen," Dylan said in a soft voice.

Quotation Marks

Double *quotation marks* are used to at the beginning and end of a direct quote. They are also used with certain titles and to indicate that a term being used is slang or referenced in the sentence. Quotation marks should not be used with an indirect quote. Single quotation marks are used to indicate a quote within a quote.

> Direct quote: "The weather is supposed to be beautiful this week," she said.

> Indirect quote: One of the customers asked if the sale prices were still in effect.

> Quote within a quote: "My little boy just said 'Mama, I want cookie,'" Maria shared.

Titles: Quotation marks should also be used to indicate titles of short works or sections of larger works, such as chapter titles. Other works that use quotation marks include poems, short stories, newspaper articles, magazine articles, web page titles, and songs.

> "The Road Not Taken" is my favorite poem by Robert Frost.

> "What a Wonderful World" is one of my favorite songs.

Specific or emphasized terms: Quotation marks can also be used to indicate a technical term or to set off a word that is being discussed in a sentence. Quotation marks can also indicate sarcasm.

> The new step, called "levigation", is a very difficult technique.

> He said he was "hungry" multiple times, but he only ate two bites.

Use with other punctuation: The use of quotation marks with other punctuation varies, depending on the role of the ending or separating punctuation.

In American English, *periods* and *commas* always go inside the quotation marks:

> "This is the last time you are allowed to leave early," his boss stated.

> The newscaster said, "We have some breaking news to report."

Question marks or *exclamation points* go inside the quotation marks when they are part of a direct quote:

> The doctor shouted, "Get the crash cart!"

When the question mark or exclamation point is part of the sentence, not the quote, it should be placed outside of the quotation marks:

> Was it Jackie that said, "Get some potatoes at the store"?

Apostrophes

This punctuation mark, the apostrophe (') is a versatile mark. It has several different functions:

- Quotes: Apostrophes are used when a second quote is needed within a quote.

  > In my letter to my friend, I wrote, "The girl had to get a new purse, and guess what Mary did? She said, 'I'd like to go with you to the store.' I knew Mary would buy it for her."

- Contractions: Another use for an apostrophe in the quote above is a contraction. *I'd* is used for *I would.*

- Possession: An apostrophe followed by the letter s shows possession (Mary's purse). If the possessive word is plural, the apostrophe generally just follows the word. Not all possessive pronouns require apostrophes.

  > The trees' leaves are all over the ground.

Hyphens

The *hyphen* (-) is a small hash mark that can be used to join words to show that they are linked.

Hyphenate two words that work together as a single adjective (a compound adjective).

> honey-covered biscuits

Some words always require hyphens, even if not serving as an adjective.

> merry-go-round

Hyphens always go after certain prefixes like *anti-* & *all-*.

Hyphens should also be used when the absence of the hyphen would cause a strange vowel combination (*semi-engineer*) or confusion. For example, *re-collect* should be used to describe something being gathered twice rather than being written as *recollect*, which means to remember.

Subjects

Every sentence must include a subject and a verb. The *subject* of a sentence is who or what the sentence is about. It's often directly stated and can be determined by asking "Who?" or "What?" did the action:

Most sentences contain a direct subject, in which the subject is mentioned in the sentence.

> *Kelly mowed the lawn.*

> Who mowed the lawn? *Kelly*

> *The air-conditioner ran all night*

> What ran all night? *the air-conditioner*

The subject of imperative sentences is *you*, because imperative subjects are commands. the subject is implied because it is a command:

> *Go home after the meeting.*

> Who should go home after the meeting? *you* (implied)

In *expletive sentences* that start with "there are" or "there is," the subject is found after the predicate. The subject cannot be "there," so it must be another word in the sentence:

> *There is a cup sitting on the coffee table.*

> What is sitting on the coffee table? *a cup*

Simple and Complete Subjects

A *complete subject* includes the simple subject and all the words modifying it, including articles and adjectives. A *simple subject* is the single noun without its modifiers.

> A warm, chocolate-chip cookie sat on the kitchen table.

> Complete subject: *a warm, chocolate-chip cookie*

> Simple subject: *cookie*

The words *a, warm, chocolate,* and *chip* all modify the simple subject *cookie*.

There might also be a *compound subject*, which would be two or more nouns without the modifiers.

> A little girl and her mother walked into the shop.

> Complete subject: *A little girl and her mother*

> Compound subject: *girl, mother*

In this case, *the girl and her mother* are both completing the action of walking into the shop, so this is a *compound subject*.

Predicates

In addition to the subject, a sentence must also have a predicate. The *predicate* contains a verb and tells something about the subject. In addition to the verb, a predicate can also contain a direct or indirect object, object of a preposition, and other phrases.

> The cats napped on the front porch.

In this sentence, *cats* is the subject because they are who or what the sentence is about.

The *complete predicate* is everything else in the sentence: *napped on the front porch.* This phrase is the predicate because it tells us what the cats did.

This sentence can be broken down into a simple subject and predicate:

> Cats napped.

In this sentence, *cats* is the simple subject, and *napped* is the *simple predicate*.

Although the sentence is very short and doesn't offer much information, it's still considered a complete sentence because it contains a subject and predicate.

Like a compound subject, a sentence can also have a **compound predicate**. This is when the subject is or does two or more things in the sentence.

> This easy chair reclines and swivels.

In this sentence, *this easy chair* is the complete subject. *Reclines and swivels* shows two actions of the chair, so this is the compound predicate.

Subject-Verb Agreement

The subject of a sentence and its verb must agree. The cornerstone rule of subject-verb agreement is that subject and verb must agree in number. Whether the subject is singular or plural, the verb must follow suit.

> Incorrect: The houses is new.
> Correct: The houses are new.
> Also Correct: The house is new.

> In other words, a singular subject requires a singular verb; a plural subject requires a plural verb.

The words or phrases that come between the subject and verb do not alter this rule.

    Incorrect: The houses built of brick is new.
    Correct: The houses built of brick are new.

    Incorrect: The houses with the sturdy porches is new.
    Correct: The houses with the sturdy porches are new.

The subject will always follow the verb when a sentence begins with *here* or *there*. Identify these with care.

    Incorrect: Here *is* the *houses* with sturdy porches.
    Correct: Here *are* the *houses* with sturdy porches.

The subject in the sentences above is not *here*, it is *houses*. Remember, *here* and *there* are never subjects. Be careful that contractions such as *here's* or *there're* do not cause confusion!

Two subjects joined by *and* require a plural verb form, except when the two combine to make one thing:

    Incorrect: Garrett and Jonathan is over there.
    Correct: Garrett and Jonathan are over there.

    Incorrect: Spaghetti and meatballs are a delicious meal!
    Correct: Spaghetti and meatballs is a delicious meal!

In the example above, *spaghetti and meatballs* is a compound noun. However, *Garrett and Jonathan* is not a compound noun.

Two singular subjects joined by *or, either/or,* or *neither/nor* call for a singular verb form.

    Incorrect: Butter or syrup are acceptable.
    Correct: Butter or syrup is acceptable.

Plural subjects joined by *or, either/or,* or *neither/nor* are, indeed, plural.

    The chairs or the boxes are being moved next.

If one subject is singular and the other is plural, the verb should agree with the closest noun.

    Correct: The chair or the boxes are being moved next.
    Correct: The chairs or the box is being moved next.

Some plurals of money, distance, and time call for a singular verb.

    Incorrect: Three dollars *are* enough to buy that.
    Correct: Three dollars *is* enough to buy that.

For words declaring degrees of quantity such as *many of, some of,* or *most of,* let the noun that follows *of* be the guide:.

    Incorrect: Many of the books is in the shelf.
    Correct: Many of the books are in the shelf.

Incorrect: Most of the pie *are* on the table.
Correct: Most of the pie *is* on the table.

For indefinite pronouns like anybody or everybody, use singular verbs.

Everybody *is* going to the store.

However, the pronouns *few, many, several, all, some,* and *both* have their own rules and use plural forms.

Some *are* ready.

Some nouns like *crowd* and *congress* are called *collective nouns* and they require a singular verb form.

Congress *is* in session.
The news *is* over.

Books and movie titles, though, including plural nouns such as *Great Expectations*, also require a singular verb. Remember that only the subject affects the verb. While writing tricky subject-verb arrangements, say them aloud. Listen to them. Once the rules have been learned, one's ear will become sensitive to them, making it easier to pick out what's right and what's wrong.

Direct Objects

The *direct object* is the part of the sentence that receives the action of the verb. It is a noun and can usually be found after the verb. To find the direct object, first find the verb, and then ask the question *who* or *what* after it.

The bear climbed the tree.

What did the bear climb? *the tree*

Indirect Objects

An *indirect object* receives the direct object. It is usually found between the verb and the direct object. A strategy for identifying the indirect object is to find the verb and ask the questions *to whom/for whom* or *to what/ for what.*

Jane made her daughter a cake.

For whom did Jane make the cake? *her daughter*

Cake is the direct object because it is what Jane made, and *daughter* is the indirect object because she receives the cake.

Complements

A *complement* completes the meaning of an expression. A complement can be a pronoun, noun, or adjective. A verb complement refers to the direct object or indirect object in the sentence. An object complement gives more information about the direct object:

The magician got the kids excited.

Kids is the direct object, and *excited* is the object complement.

A *subject complement* comes after a linking verb. It is typically an adjective or noun that gives more information about the subject:

The king was noble and spared the thief's life.

Noble describes the *king* and follows the linking verb *was*.

Predicate Nouns

A *predicate noun* renames the subject:

John is a carpenter.

The subject is *John*, and the predicate noun is *carpenter*.

Predicate Adjectives

A *predicate adjective* describes the subject:

Margaret is beautiful.

The subject is *Margaret*, and the predicate adjective is *beautiful*.

Homonyms

Homonyms are words that sound the same but are spelled differently, and they have different meanings. There are several common homonyms that give writers trouble.

There, *They're*, and *Their*
The word *there* can be used as an adverb, adjective, or pronoun:

There are ten children on the swim team this summer.

I put my book over *there*, but now I can't find it.

The word *they're* is a contraction of the words *they* and *are*:

They're flying in from Texas on Tuesday.

The word *their* is a possessive pronoun:

I store *their* winter clothes in the attic.

Its and *It's*

Its is a possessive pronoun:

>The cat licked *its* injured paw.

It's is the contraction for the words *it* and *is*:

>*It's* unbelievable how many people opted not to vote in the last election.

Your and You're
Your is a possessive pronoun:

>Can I borrow *your* lawnmower this weekend?

You're is a contraction for the words *you* and *are*:

>*You're* about to embark on a fantastic journey.

To, Too, and Two
To is an adverb or a preposition used to show direction, relationship, or purpose:

>We are going *to* New York.

>They are going *to* see a show.

Too is an adverb that means more than enough, also, and very:

>You have had *too* much candy.

>We are on vacation that week, *too*.

Two is the written-out form of the numeral 2:

>*Two* of the shirts didn't fit, so I will have to return them.

New and Knew
New is an adjective that means recent:

>There's a *new* customer on the phone.

Knew is the past tense of the verb *know*:

>I *knew* you'd have fun on this ride.

Affect and *Effect*

Affect and *effect* are complicated because they are used as both nouns and verbs, have similar meanings, and are pronounced the same.

	Affect	**Effect**
Noun Definition	emotional state	result
Noun Example	The patient's affect was flat.	The effects of smoking are well documented.
Verb Definition	to influence	to bring about
Verb Example	The pollen count affects my allergies.	The new candidate hopes to effect change.

Independent and Dependent Clauses

Independent and *dependent* clauses are strings of words that contain both a subject and a verb. An independent clause *can* stand alone as complete thought, but a dependent clause *cannot*. A dependent clause relies on other words to be a complete sentence.

> Independent clause: The keys are on the counter.
> Dependent clause: If the keys are on the counter

Notice that both clauses have a subject (*keys*) and a verb (*are*). The independent clause expresses a complete thought, but the word *if* at the beginning of the dependent clause makes it *dependent* on other words to be a complete thought.

> Independent clause: If the keys are on the counter, please give them to me.

This presents a complete sentence since it includes at least one verb and one subject and is a complete thought. In this case, the independent clause has two subjects (*keys* & an implied *you*) and two verbs (*are* & *give*).

> Independent clause: I went to the store.
> Dependent clause: Because we are out of milk,
>
> Complete Sentence: Because we are out of milk, I went to the store.
> Complete Sentence: I went to the store because we are out of milk.

Phrases

A *phrase* is a group of words that do not make a complete thought or a clause. They are parts of sentences or clauses. Phrases can be used as nouns, adjectives, or adverbs. A phrase does not contain both a subject and a verb.

Prepositional Phrases

A *prepositional phrase* shows the relationship between a word in the sentence and the object of the preposition. The object of the preposition is a noun that follows the preposition.

> The orange pillows are on the couch.

On is the preposition, and *couch* is the object of the preposition.

> She brought her friend with the nice car.

With is the preposition, and *car* is the object of the preposition. Here are some common prepositions:

about	as	at	after
by	for	from	in
of	on	to	with

Verbals and Verbal Phrases

Verbals are forms of verbs that act as other parts of speech. They can be used as nouns, adjectives, or adverbs. Though they are use verb forms, they are not to be used as the verb in the sentence. A word group that is based on a verbal is considered a *verbal phrase*. There are three major types of verbals: *participles, gerunds,* and *infinitives.*

Participles are verbals that act as adjectives. The present participle ends in *–ing,* and the past participle ends in *–d, -ed, -n,* or *-t.*

Verb	Present Participle	Past Participle
walk	walking	walked
share	sharing	shared

Participial phrases are made up of the participle and modifiers, complements, or objects.

Crying for most of an hour, the baby didn't seem to want to nap.

Having already taken this course, the student was bored during class.

Crying for most of an hour and *Having already taken this course* are the participial phrases.

Gerunds are verbals that are used as nouns and end in *–ing.* A gerund can be the subject or object of the sentence like a noun. Note that a present participle can also end in *–ing,* so it is important to distinguish between the two. The gerund is used as a noun, while the participle is used as an adjective.

Swimming is my favorite sport.

I wish I were sleeping.

A *gerund phrase* includes the gerund and any modifiers or complements, direct objects, indirect objects, or pronouns.

Cleaning the house is my least favorite weekend activity.

Cleaning the house is the gerund phrase acting as the subject of the sentence.

The most important goal this year is raising money for charity.

Raising money for charity is the gerund phrase acting as the direct object.

The police accused the woman of stealing the car.

The *gerund* phrase *stealing the car* is the object of the preposition in this sentence.

An *infinitive* is a verbal made up of the word to and a verb. Infinitives can be used as nouns, adjectives, or adverbs.

Examples: To eat, to jump, to swim, to lie, to call, to work

An *infinitive phrase* is made up of the infinitive plus any complements or modifiers. The infinitive phrase *to wait* is used as the subject in this sentence:

To wait was not what I had in mind.

The infinitive phrase *to sing* is used as the subject complement in this sentence:

Her dream is to sing.

The infinitive phrase *to grow* is used as an adverb in this sentence:

Children must eat to grow.

Appositive Phrases

An *appositive* is a noun or noun phrase that renames a noun that comes immediately before it in the sentence. An appositive can be a single word or several words. These phrases can be *essential* or *nonessential*. An essential appositive phrase is necessary to the meaning of the sentence and a nonessential appositive phrase is not. It is important to be able to distinguish these for purposes of comma use.

Essential: My sister Christina works at a school.

Naming which sister is essential to the meaning of the sentence, so no commas are needed.

Nonessential: My sister, who is a teacher, is coming over for dinner tonight.

Who is a teacher is not essential to the meaning of the sentence, so commas are required.

Absolute Phrases

An *absolute phrase* modifies a noun without using a conjunction. It is not the subject of the sentence and is not a complete thought on its own. Absolute phrases are set off from the independent clause with a comma.

Arms outstretched, she yelled at the sky.

All things considered, this has been a great day.

The Four Types of Sentence Structures

A *simple sentence* has one independent clause.

I am going to win.

A *compound sentence* has two independent clauses. A conjunction—*for, and, nor, but, or, yet, so*—links them together. Note that each of the independent clauses has a subject and a verb.

> I am going to win, but the odds are against me.

A *complex sentence* has one independent clause and one or more dependent clauses.

> I am going to win, even though I don't deserve it.

Even though I don't deserve it is a dependent clause. It does not stand on its own. Some conjunctions that link an independent and a dependent clause are *although, because, before, after, that, when, which,* and *while*.

A *compound-complex sentence* has at least three clauses, two of which are independent and at least one that is a dependent clause.

While trying to dance, I tripped over my partner's feet, but I regained my balance quickly.

> The dependent clause is *While trying to dance*.

Sentence Fragments

A *sentence fragment* is an incomplete sentence. An independent clause is made up of a subject and a predicate, and both are needed to make a complete sentence.

Sentence fragments are often begin with *relative pronouns* (when, which*), subordinating conjunctions* (because, although*) or *gerunds* (trying, being, seeing). They might be missing the subject or the predicate.

The most common type of fragment is the isolated dependent clause, which can be corrected by joining it to the independent clause that appears before or after the fragment:

> Fragment: While the cookies baked.

> Correction: While the cookies baked, we played cards. (We played cards while the cookies baked.)

Run-on Sentences

A *run-on sentence* is created when two independent clauses (complete thoughts) are joined without correct punctuation or a conjunction. Run-on sentences can be corrected in the following ways:

- Join the independent clauses with a comma and coordinating conjunction.

> Run-on: We forgot to return the library books we had to pay a fine.

> Correction: We forgot to return the library books, so we had to pay a fine.

- Join the independent clauses with a semicolon, dash, or colon when the clauses are closely related in meaning.

  Run-on: I had a salad for lunch every day this week I feel healthier already.

  Correction: I had a salad for lunch every day this week; I feel healthier already.

- Join the independent clauses with a *semicolon and a conjunctive adverb.*

  Run-on: We arrived at the animal shelter on time however the dog had already been adopted.

  Correction: We arrived at the animal shelter on time; however, the dog had already been adopted.

- Separate the independent clauses into two sentences *with a period.*

  Run-on: He tapes his favorite television show he never misses an episode.

  Correction: He tapes his favorite television show. He never misses an episode.

- *Rearrange the wording* of the sentence to create an independent clause and a dependent clause.

  Run-on: My wedding date is coming up I am getting more excited to walk down the aisle.

  Correction: As my wedding date approaches, I am getting more excited to walk down the aisle.

Dangling and Misplaced Modifiers

A *modifier* is a phrase that describes, alters, limits, or gives more information about a word in the sentence. The two most common issues are dangling and misplaced modifiers.

A *dangling modifier* is created when the phrase modifies a word that is not clearly stated in the sentence.

  Dangling modifier: Having finished dinner, the dishes were cleared from the table.

  Correction: Having finished dinner, Amy cleared the dishes from the table.

In the first sentence, *having finished dinner* appears to modify *the dishes*, which obviously can't finish dinner. The second sentence adds the subject *Amy*, to make it clear who has finished dinner.

  Dangling modifier: Hoping to improve test scores, all new books were ordered for the school.

  Correction: Hoping to improve test scores, administrators ordered all new books for the school.

Without the subject *administrators*, it appears the books are hoping to improve test scores, which doesn't make sense.

Misplaced modifiers are placed incorrectly in the sentence, which can cause confusion. Compare these examples:

> Misplaced modifier: Rory purchased a new flat screen television and placed it on the wall above the fireplace, with all the bells and whistles.

> Revised: Rory purchased a new flat screen television, with all the bells and whistles, and placed it on the wall above the fireplace.

The bells and whistles should modify the television, not the fireplace.

> Misplaced modifier: The delivery driver arrived late with the pizza, who was usually on time.

> Revised: The delivery driver, who usually was on time, arrived late with the pizza.

This suggests that the delivery driver was usually on time, instead of the pizza.

> Misplaced modifier: We saw a family of ducks on the way to church.

> Revised: On the way to church, we saw a family of ducks.

> The misplaced modifier, here, suggests the *ducks* were on their way to church, instead of the pronoun *we*.

Split Infinitives

An infinitive is made up of the word *to* and a verb, such as: to run, to jump, to ask. A *split infinitive* is created when a word comes between *to* and the verb.

> Split infinitive: To quickly run

> Correction: To run quickly

> Split infinitive: To quietly ask

> Correction: To ask quietly

Double Negatives

A *double negative* is a negative statement that includes two negative elements. This is incorrect in Standard English.

> Incorrect: She hasn't never come to my house to visit.

> Correct: She has never come to my house to visit.

The intended meaning is that she has never come to the house, so the double negative is incorrect. However, it is possible to use two negatives to create a positive statement.

> Correct: She was not unhappy with her performance on the quiz.

In this case, the double negative, *was not unhappy*, is intended to show a positive, so it is correct. This means that she was somewhat happy with her performance.

Faulty Parallelism

It is necessary to use parallel construction in sentences that have multiple similar ideas. Using parallel structure provides clarity in writing. *Faulty parallelism* is created when multiple ideas are joined using different sentence structures. Compare these examples:

Incorrect: We start each practice with stretches, a run, and fielding grounders.
Correct: We start each practice with stretching, running, and fielding grounders.

Incorrect: I watched some television, reading my book, and fell asleep.
Correct: I watched some television, read my book, and fell asleep.

Incorrect: *Some of the readiness skills for Kindergarten are to cut with scissors, to tie shoes, and dressing independently.*
Correct: *Some of the readiness skills for Kindergarten are being able to cut with scissors, to tie shoes, and to dress independently.*

Subordination

If multiple pieces of information in a sentence are not equal, they can be joined by creating an independent clause and a dependent clause. The less important information becomes the *subordinate clause*:

Draft: The hotel was acceptable. We wouldn't stay at the hotel again.

Revised: Though the hotel was acceptable, we wouldn't stay there again.

The more important information (*we wouldn't stay there again*) becomes the main clause, and the less important information (*the hotel was acceptable*) becomes the subordinate clause.

Context Clues

Context clues help readers understand unfamiliar words, and thankfully, there are many types.

Synonyms are words or phrases that have nearly, if not exactly, the same meaning as other words or phrases

Large boxes are needed to pack *big* items.

Antonyms are words or phrases that have opposite definitions. Antonyms, like synonyms, can serve as context clues, although more cryptically.

Large boxes are not needed to pack *small* items.

Definitions are sometimes included within a sentence to define uncommon words.

They practiced the *rumba, a type of dance,* for hours on end.

Explanations provide context through elaboration.

Large boxes holding items weighing over 60 pounds were stacked in the corner.

Here's an example of *contrast*:

These *minute* creatures were much different than the *huge* mammals that the zoologist was accustomed to dealing with.

Beware of Simplicity

Sometimes the answer may seem very simple. In this case, it's prudent to look more carefully at the question and the possible answer choices. Very brief answers aren't always correct, and the opposite may also be true. The goal is to read all the answer choices carefully, trying to rule out those that don't make sense.

Final Notes

It's best to read every answer choice before making a decision. While some answers may seem plausible, there may be others that are better choices. First instinct is usually right, but reading every answer is recommended. Caution should be taken in choosing an answer that "sounds right." Grammar rules can be tricky, and what sounds right may not be correct. It's best to rely on knowledge of grammar to choose the best answer. Ruling out incorrect responses can help narrow the choices down. Choosing between two choices (after reading them carefully) and selecting the answer that best matches the rules of Standard English is less overwhelming.

Practice Questions

Sentence Correction

Directions for questions 1–10

Select the best version of the underlined part of the sentence. The first choice is the same as the original sentence. If you think the original sentence is best, choose the first answer.

1. <u>An important issues stemming from this meeting</u> is that we won't have enough time to meet all of the objectives.
    a. An important issues stemming from this meeting
    b. Important issue stemming from this meeting
    c. An important issue stemming from this meeting
    d. Important issues stemming from this meeting

2. The rising popularity of the clean eating movement can be attributed <u>to the fact that experts say added sugars and chemicals in our food are to blame for the obesity epidemic.</u>
    a. to the fact that experts say added sugars and chemicals in our food are to blame for the obesity epidemic.
    b. in the facts that experts say added sugars and chemicals in our food are to blame for the obesity epidemic.
    c. to the fact that experts saying added sugars and chemicals in our food are to blame for the obesity epidemic.
    d. with the facts that experts say added sugars and chemicals in our food are to blame for the obesity epidemic.

3. She's looking for a suitcase that can fit all of her <u>clothes, shoes, accessory, and makeup.</u>
    a. clothes, shoes, accessory, and makeup.
    b. clothes, shoes, accessories, and makeup.
    c. clothes, shoes, accessories, and makeups.
    d. clothes, shoe, accessory, and makeup.

4. <u>Because Shaun was used to playing guitar,</u> he needs to work much harder at playing bass.
    a. Because Shaun was used to playing guitar,
    b. Even though Shaun is used to playing guitar,
    c. While Shaun was used to playing guitar,
    d. Because Shaun is used to playing guitar,

5. <u>Considering the recent rains we have had, it's a wonder</u> the plants haven't drowned.
    a. Considering the recent rains we have had, it's a wonder
    b. Consider the recent rains we have had, it's a wonder
    c. Considering for how much recent rain we have had, its a wonder
    d. Considering, the recent rains we have had, its a wonder

6. <u>Since none of the furniture were delivered on time,</u> we have to move in at a later date.
   a. Since none of the furniture were delivered on time,
   b. Since none of the furniture was delivered on time,
   c. Since all of the furniture were delivered on time,
   d. Since all of the furniture was delivered on time

7. It is necessary for instructors to offer tutoring <u>to any students who need extra help in the class.</u>
   a. to any students who need extra help in the class.
   b. for any students that need extra help in the class.
   c. with any students who need extra help in the class.
   d. for any students needing any extra help in their class.

8. The fact the <u>train set only includes four cars and one small track was a big disappointment</u> to my son.
   a. the train set only includes four cars and one small track was a big disappointment
   b. that the trains set only include four cars and one small track was a big disappointment
   c. that the train set only includes four cars and one small track was a big disappointment
   d. that the train set only includes four cars and one small track were a big disappointment

9. <u>Because many people</u> feel there are too many distractions to get any work done, I actually enjoy working from home.
   a. Because many people
   b. While many people
   c. Maybe many people
   d. With most people

10. There were many questions <u>about what causes the case to have gone cold</u>, but the detective wasn't willing to discuss it with reporters.
   a. about what causes the case to have gone cold
   b. about why the case is cold
   c. about what causes the case to go cold
   d. about why the case went cold

Construction Shift

Directions for questions 11–20

Rewrite the sentence in your head following the directions given below. Keep in mind that your new sentence should be well written and should have essentially the same meaning as the original sentence.

11. Although she was nervous speaking in front of a crowd, the author read her narrative with poise and confidence.

Rewrite, beginning with

<u>The author had poise and confidence while reading</u>

The next words will be
   a. because she was nervous speaking in front of a crowd.
   b. but she was nervous speaking in front of a crowd.
   c. even though she was nervous speaking in front of a crowd.
   d. before she was nervous speaking in front of a crowd.

12. There was a storm surge and loss of electricity during the hurricane.

Rewrite, beginning with

<u>While the hurricane occurred,</u>

The next words will be
    a. there was a storm surge after the electricity went out.
    b. the storm surge caused the electricity to go out.
    c. the electricity surged into the storm.
    d. the electricity went out and there was a storm surge.

13. When one elephant in a herd is sick, the rest of the herd will help it walk and bring it food.

Rewrite, beginning with

<u>An elephant herd will</u>

The next words will be
    a. be too sick and tired to walk
    b. help and support
    c. gather food when they're sick
    d. be unable to walk without food

14. They went out to eat after the soccer game.

Rewrite, beginning with

<u>They finished the soccer game</u>

The next words will be
    a. then went out to eat.
    b. after they went out to eat.
    c. so they could go out to eat.
    d. because they went out to eat.

15. Armani got lost when she walked around Paris.

Rewrite, beginning with

<u>Walking through Paris,</u>

The next words will be
    a. you can get lost.
    b. Armani found herself lost.
    c. she should have gotten lost.
    d. is about getting lost.

16. After his cat died, Phoenix buried the cat with her favorite toys in his backyard.

Rewrite, beginning with

Phoenix buried his cat

The next words will be
    a. in his backyard before she died.
    b. after she died in the backyard.
    c. with her favorite toys after she died.
    d. after he buried her toys in the backyard.

17. While I was in the helicopter I saw the sunset, and tears streamed down my eyes.

Rewrite, beginning with

Tears streamed down my eyes

The next words will be:
    a. while I watched the helicopter fly into the sunset.
    b. because the sunset flew up into the sky.
    c. because the helicopter was facing the sunset.
    d. when I saw the sunset from the helicopter.

18. I won't go to the party unless some of my friends go.

Rewrite, beginning with

I will go the party

The next words will be
    a. if I want to.
    b. if my friends go.
    c. since a couple of my friends are going.
    d. unless people I know go.

19. He had a broken leg before the car accident, so it took him a long time to recover.

Rewrite, beginning with

He took a long time to recover from the car accident

The next words will be
    a. from his two broken legs.
    b. after he broke his leg.
    c. because he already had a broken leg.
    d. since he broke his leg again afterward.

20. We had a party the day after Halloween to celebrate my birthday.

Rewrite, beginning with

It was my birthday.

The next words will be
  a. , so we celebrated with a party the day after Halloween.
  b. the day of Halloween so we celebrated with a party.
  c. , and we celebrated with a Halloween party the day after.
  d. a few days before Halloween, so we threw a party.

Answer Explanations

Sentence Correction

1. C: In this answer, the article and subject agree, and the subject and predicate agree. Choice *C* is incorrect because the article (*an*) and the noun (*issues*) do not agree in number. Choice *B* is incorrect because an article is needed before *important issue*. Choice *D* is incorrect because the plural subject *issues* does not agree with the singular verb *is*.

2. A: Choices *B* and *D* both use the expression *attributed to the fact* incorrectly. It can only be attributed *to* the fact, not *with* or *in* the fact. Choice *C* incorrectly uses a gerund, *saying*, when it should use the present tense of the verb *say*.

3. B: Choice *B* is correct because it uses correct parallel structure of plural nouns. *A* is incorrect because the word *accessory* is in singular form. Choice *C* is incorrect because it pluralizes *makeup*, which is already in plural form. Choice *D* is incorrect because it again uses the singular *accessory*, and it uses the singular *shoe*.

4. D: In a cause/effect relationship, it is correct to begin with the word *because*. This can eliminate both Choices *B* and *C*, which don't clearly show the cause/effect relationship. Choice *A* is incorrect because it uses the past tense, when the main clause is in the present tense. It makes grammatical sense for both parts of the sentence to be in present tense.

5. A: In Choice *B*, the present tense form of the verb *consider* creates an independent clause joined to another independent clause with only a comma, which is a comma splice and grammatically incorrect. Both *C* and *D* use the possessive form of *its*, when it should be the contraction *it's* for *it is*. Choice *D* also includes incorrect comma placement.

6. B: Choice *A* uses the plural form of the verb, when the subject is the pronoun *none*, which needs a singular verb. Choice *C* also uses the wrong verb form and uses the word *all* in place of *none*, which doesn't make sense in the context of the sentence. Choice *D* uses *all* again, and is missing the comma, which is necessary to set the dependent clause off from the independent clause.

7. A: Answer Choice *A* uses the best, most concise word choice. Choice *B* uses the pronoun *that* to refer to people instead of *who*. *C* incorrectly uses the preposition *with*. Choice *D* uses the preposition *for* and the additional word *any*, making the sentence wordy and less clear.

8. C: Choice *A* is missing the word *that*, which is necessary for the sentence to make sense. Choice *B* pluralizes *trains* and uses the singular form of the word *include*, so it does not agree with the word *set*. Choice *D* changes the verb to *were*, which is in plural form and does not agree with the singular subject.

9. B: Choice *B* uses the best choice of words to create a subordinate and independent clause. In Choice *B*, *because* makes it seem like this is the reason I enjoy working from home, which is incorrect. In *C*, the word *maybe* creates two independent clauses, which are not joined properly with a comma. Choice *D* uses *with*, which does not make grammatical sense.

10. D: Choices *A* and *C* use additional words and phrases that are not necessary. Choice *B* is more concise, but uses the present tense of *is*. This does not agree with the rest of the sentence, which uses past tense. The best choice is Choice *D*, which uses the most concise sentence structure and is grammatically correct.

Construction Shift

11. C: The original sentence states that despite the author being nervous, she was able to read with poise and confidence, which is stated in Choice *C*. Choice *A* changes the meaning by adding *because*; however, the author didn't read with confidence *because* she was nervous, but *despite* being nervous. Choice *B* is closer to the original meaning; however, it loses the emphasis of her succeeding *despite* her condition. Choice *D* adds the word *before*, which doesn't make much sense on its own, much less in relation to the original sentence.

12. D: The original sentence states that there was a storm surge and loss of electricity during the hurricane, making Choice *D* correct. Choices *A* and *B* arrange the storm surge and the loss of electricity within a cause and effect statement, which changes the meaning of the original sentence. Choice *C* changes *surge* from a noun into a verb and creates an entirely different situation.

13. B: The original sentence states that an elephant herd will help and support another herd member if it is sick, so Choice *B* is correct. Choice *A* is incorrect because it states the whole herd will be too sick and too tired to walk instead of a single elephant. Choice *C* is incorrect because the original sentence does not say that the herd gathers food when *they* are sick, but when a single member of the herd is sick. Although Choice *D* might be correct in a general sense, it does not relate to the meaning of the original sentence and is therefore incorrect.

14. A: The original sentence says that after a soccer game, they went out to eat. Choice *A* shows the same sequence: they finished the soccer game *then* went out to eat. Choice *B* is incorrect because it reverses the sequence of events. Choices *C* and *D* are incorrect because the words *so* and *because* change the meaning of the original sentence.

15. B: Choice *B* arggis correct because the idea of the original sentences is Armani getting lost while walking through Paris. Choice *A* is incorrect because it replaces third person with second person. Choice *C* is incorrect because the word *should* indicates an obligation to get lost. Choice *D* is incorrect because it is not specific to the original sentence but instead makes a generalization about getting lost.

16. C: Choice *C* is correct because it shows that Phoenix buried his cat with her favorite toys after she died, which is true of the original statement. Although Choices *A*, *B*, and *D* mention a backyard, the meanings of these choices are skewed. Choice *A* says that Phoenix buried his cat alive, which is incorrect. Choice *B* says his cat died in the backyard, which we do not know to be true. Choice *D* says Phoenix buried his cat after he buried her toys, which is also incorrect.

17. D: Choice *D* is correct because it expresses the sentiment of a moment of joy bringing tears to one's eyes as one sees a sunset while in a helicopter. Choice *A* is incorrect because it implies that the person was outside of the helicopter watching it from afar. Choice *B* is incorrect because the original sentence does not portray the sunset *flying up* into the sky. Choice *C* is incorrect because, while the helicopter may have been facing the sunset, this is not the reason that tears were in the speaker's eyes.

18. B: *B* is correct because like the original sentence, it expresses their plan to go to the party if friends also go. Choice *A* is incorrect because it does not follow the meaning of the original sentence. Choice *C* is incorrect because it states that their friends are going, even though that is not known. Choice D is incorrect because it would make the new sentence mean the opposite of the original sentence.

19. C: Choice C is correct because the original sentence states that his recovery time was long because his leg was broken before the accident. Choice A is incorrect because there is no indication that the man had two broken legs. Choice B is incorrect because it indicates that he broke his leg during the car accident, not before. Choice D is incorrect because there is no indication that he broke his leg after the car accident.

20. A: Choice A is correct because it expresses the fact that the birthday and the party were both after Halloween. Choice B is incorrect because it says that the birthday was on Halloween, even though that was not stated in the original sentence. Choice C is incorrect because it says the party was specifically a Halloween party and not a birthday party. Choice D is incorrect because the party was after Halloween, not before.

WriterPlacer (Written Essay)

Brainstorming

One of the most important steps in writing an essay is prewriting. Before drafting an essay, it's helpful to think about the topic for a moment or two, in order to gain a more solid understanding of what the task is. Then, spending about five minutes jotting down the immediate ideas that could work for the essay is recommended. It is a way to get some words on the page and offer a reference for ideas for when drafting. Scratch paper is provided for writers to use any prewriting techniques such as webbing, free writing, or listing. The goal is to get ideas out of the mind and onto the page.

Considering Opposing Viewpoints

In the planning stage, it's important to consider all aspects of the topic, including different viewpoints on the subject. There are more than two ways to look at a topic, and a strong argument considers those opposing viewpoints. Considering opposing viewpoints can help writers present a fair, balanced, and informed essay that shows consideration for all readers. This approach can also strengthen an argument by recognizing and potentially refuting the opposing viewpoint(s).

Drawing from personal experience may help to support ideas. For example, if the goal for writing is a personal narrative, then the story should be from the writer's own life. Many writers find it helpful to draw from personal experience, even in an essay that is not strictly narrative. Personal anecdotes or short stories can help to illustrate a point in other types of essays as well.

Moving from Brainstorming to Planning

Once the ideas are on the page, it's time to turn them into a solid plan for the essay. The best ideas from the brainstorming results can then be developed into a more formal outline. An outline typically has one main point (the thesis) and at least three sub-points that support the main point. Here's an example:

Main Idea

- Point #1
- Point #2
- Point #3

Of course, there will be details under each point, but this approach is the best for dealing with timed writing.

Staying On Track

Basing the essay on the outline aids in both organization and coherence. The goal is to ensure that there is enough time to develop each sub-point in the essay, roughly spending an equal amount of time on each idea. Keeping an eye on the time will help. If there are fifteen minutes left to draft the essay, then it makes sense to spend about 5 minutes on each of the ideas. Staying on task is critical to success, and timing out the parts of the essay can help writers avoid feeling overwhelmed.

Parts of the Essay

The *introduction* has to do a few important things:

- Establish the *topic* of the essay in original wording (i.e., not just repeating the prompt)
- Clarify the significance/importance of the topic or purpose for writing (not too many details, a brief overview)
- Offer a *thesis statement* that identifies the writer's own viewpoint on the topic (typically one-two brief sentences as a clear, concise explanation of the main point on the topic)

Body paragraphs reflect the ideas developed in the outline. Three-four points is probably sufficient for a short essay, and they should include the following:

- A *topic sentence* that identifies the sub-point (e.g., a reason why, a way how, a cause or effect)
- A detailed *explanation* of the point, explaining why the writer thinks this point is valid
- Illustrative *examples*, such as personal examples or real world examples, that support and validate the point (i.e., "prove" the point)
- A *concluding sentence* that connects the examples, reasoning, and analysis to the point being made

The *conclusion*, or final paragraph, should be brief and should reiterate the focus, clarifying why the discussion is significant or important. It is important to avoid adding specific details or new ideas to this paragraph. The purpose of the conclusion is to sum up what has been said to bring the discussion to a close.

Don't Panic!

Writing an essay can be overwhelming, and performance panic is a natural response. The outline serves as a basis for the writing and help writers keep focused. Getting stuck can also happen, and it's helpful to remember that brainstorming can be done at any time during the writing process. Following the steps of the writing process is the best defense against writer's block.

Timed essays can be particularly stressful, but assessors are trained to recognize the necessary planning and thinking for these timed efforts. Using the plan above and sticking to it helps with time management. Timing each part of the process helps writers stay on track. Sometimes writers try to cover too much in their essays. If time seems to be running out, this is an opportunity to determine whether all of the ideas in the outline are necessary. Three body paragraphs is sufficient, and more than that is probably too much to cover in a short essay.

More isn't always *better* in writing. A strong essay will be clear and concise. It will avoid unnecessary or repetitive details. It is better to have a concise, five-paragraph essay that makes a clear point, than a ten-paragraph essay that doesn't. The goal is to write one-two pages of quality writing. Paragraphs should also reflect balance; if the introduction goes to the bottom of the first page, the writing may be going off-track or be repetitive. It's best to fall into the one-two page range, but a complete, well-developed essay is the ultimate goal.

The Final Steps

Leaving a few minutes at the end to revise and proofread offers an opportunity for writers to polish things up. Putting one's self in the reader's shoes and focusing on what the essay actually says helps writers identify problems—it's a movement from the mindset of writer to the mindset of editor. The goal is to have a clean, clear copy of the essay. The following areas should be considered when proofreading:

- Sentence fragments
- Awkward sentence structure
- Run-on sentences
- Incorrect word choice
- Grammatical agreement errors
- Spelling errors
- Punctuation errors
- Capitalization errors

The Short Overview

The essay may seem challenging, but following these steps can help writers focus:

- Take one-two minutes to think about the topic.
- Generate some ideas through brainstorming (three-four minutes).
- Organize ideas into a brief outline, selecting just three-four main points to cover in the essay (eventually the body paragraphs).
- Develop essay in parts:
- Introduction paragraph, with intro to topic and main points
- Viewpoint on the subject at the end of the introduction
- Body paragraphs, based on outline
- Each paragraph: makes a main point, explains the viewpoint, uses examples to support the point
- Brief conclusion highlighting the main points and closing
- Read over the essay (last five minutes).
- Look for any obvious errors, making sure that the writing makes sense.

Practice Prompt

Prepare an essay of about 300-600 words on the topic below.

Some people feel that sharing their lives on social media sites such as Facebook, Instagram, and Snapchat is fine. They share every aspect of their lives, including pictures of themselves and their families, what they ate for lunch, who they are dating, and when they are going on vacation. They even say that if it's not on social media, it didn't happen. Other people believe that sharing so much personal information is an invasion of privacy and could prove dangerous. They think sharing personal pictures and details invites predators, cyberbullying, and identity theft.

Write an essay to someone who is considering whether to participate in social media. Take a side on the issue and argue whether or not he/she should join a social media network. Use specific examples to support your argument.

FREE Test Taking Tips DVD Offer

To help us better serve you, we have developed a Test Taking Tips DVD that we would like to give you for FREE. **This DVD covers world-class test taking tips that you can use to be even more successful when you are taking your test.**

All that we ask is that you email us your feedback about your study guide. Please let us know what you thought about it – whether that is good, bad or indifferent.

To get your **FREE Test Taking Tips DVD**, email freedvd@studyguideteam.com with "FREE DVD" in the subject line and the following information in the body of the email:

      a. The title of your study guide.

      b. Your product rating on a scale of 1-5, with 5 being the highest rating.

      c. Your feedback about the study guide. What did you think of it?

      d. Your full name and shipping address to send your free DVD.

If you have any questions or concerns, please don't hesitate to contact us at freedvd@studyguideteam.com.

Thanks again!

Made in the USA
Lexington, KY
24 March 2017